God's Purpose for Your Faith

Other Works by Al Hill

Our Evil—God's Good
And Other Sermons from Genesis through Joshua

Things That Kings Can't Do
And Other Sermons from Judges through 2ⁿᵈ Kings, and the Wisdom Books

In the Presence of the Lord
And Other Sermons from the Psalms and the Prophets

Walking with Jesus
And Other Sermons from the Gospel of Matthew

From Jerusalem to Jericho
And Other Sermons from the Gospel of Luke and the Acts of the Apostles

Traits of the Shepherd
And Other Sermons from the Gospel of John, 1ˢᵗ John and Revelation

Making Peace with Your Father
And Other Sermons from Paul's Letters to the Romans and Corinthians

The Empty God
And Other Sermons from the Shorter Letters of Paul

O Come, Let God Adore Us
And Other Sermons for Advent and Christmas

Not Exactly What They Expected
And Other Sermons for Holy Week and Easter

DEAR TRINITY
Letters from a Pastor to His People

God's Purpose for Your Faith

And Other Sermons from
Mark, Hebrews, James and 1ˢᵗ Peter

Al Hill

SOMMERTON
HOUSE

Cover design by the author.

The image on the cover of this book of Jesus raising Jairus' daughter is from a stained-glass window in St. Boniface Catholic Church in Cincinnati, Ohio, and is used with their kind permission.

ISBN: 978-1-948773-03-4 (sc)

Library of Congress Control Number: 2018902528

To learn more about, or to purchase, this or other works by Al Hill, visit www.sommertonhouse.com, or amazon.com/author/alhill.

Dedication

To our beautiful Skye,

whose sweet innocence
has brought me to
a much deeper appreciation
of what Jesus meant by
"…except you become as a little child…."

Contents

Indices

Preface

When it comes to matters of faith, most of us tend to think in terms of *"our* faith"—what *we* believe about God, and what *we* think about what's right and wrong, and how *we* see ourselves as moral actors, and in relation to God. We live in an age and a culture where matters of faith are considered to be personal matters—and for many people, private matters: "What I 'believe' is my business, and how I 'practice my faith' is my business. Nobody—and no 'body' (whether congregational or denominational)—has the right or authority to tell me what I should believe or what I should or shouldn't do."

That's more or less where most of us are today.

But suppose we've got this personal faith business all wrong? Suppose faith—*our* faith—is not something that belongs to us individually and over which we have the final say, to do with as we please. And suppose we bypass the discussion of "intermediate" spiritual or moral authority altogether right now and just consider the issue of "ultimaticity," or whatever the appropriate word is. Suppose our faith, and all that goes with it, belongs, not to us, but to God, because He created it, just like He created everything else.

The biblical perspective has always been that God created all things—and therefore us and everything about us (except sin). And so, therefore, He created our capacity for faith—intentionally, rather than accidentally. And if that is so, there was and is a divine purpose for us and our faith, just as there was and is for everything God brought and brings into existence.

I suspect that few people ever give a thought to the possibility that the part of us that contains the capacity for faith has a divinely-determined purpose. At best, we tend to think in terms of what we "get out of" our faith—how we fall back on it in hard times for emotional support—though we ignore it, or assume it unthinkingly, when things seem all right.

But if the faith in us merely resides in us without our "owning" it—and actually belongs to Someone else who put it there for His purpose in the first place—*His* purpose for our faith ought to be something we should think about. *His* would be the prior claim on our faith and take precedence over any purpose (or no purpose) we may have conceived for it.

What does God want our faith to accomplish in us, and how do we find that out, and how do we contribute to the accomplishment of that purpose? Considering that question is what the title sermon in this book attempts to do. In fact, I hope you will find that all the sermons in this collection will have addressed the question of our faith's purpose in some way.

�❧

You will notice that the first three sermons in this collection are all based on the same brief passage in Mark, Chapter 1—and the second and third, especially, have a lot of overlapping. (Okay, they're almost the same sermon.) Maybe we could just call them "synoptic sermons," since, like the first three Gospels, they draw on the same materials, and in several places, are the same, word for word.

I decided to include all three to show that a sermon can be repeated—or better, "developed"—after it has been preached the first time. And, to be frank, I did not know which version you would find the most useful. There is a similar duplication in the three sermons from Mark 6, verses 30 and following.

❧

Let me also address some matters of style and organization in the pages that follow. Throughout the book, you will find that pronouns and other words referring to Father, Son or Holy Ghost/Spirit have been capitalized, though this is no longer the general convention. I capitalize these divine pronouns and referents as a personal expression of reverence (practiced since childhood)—but the practice also serves in a number of places to reduce confusion about the persons (or Persons) to whom (or Whom) multiple pronouns refer. The exceptions to my "personal capitalization policy" are in the copyrighted translations of the Bible, which are reprinted as published.

I have provided footnotes that did not exist in the original, oral presentations. When passages from the Bible are quoted, the version is identified in the footnote. When I have paraphrased scripture—or felt that biblical support was appropriate for some affirmation or allusion in the sermon—I have indicated the passage in a footnote without specifying a version.

To assist other preachers and those who might want to maneuver more readily around the material, I have provided a quartet of indices in the back. I often wished I had had such indices in the books of sermons I used for study and inspiration over the years, and I hope these "helps" will prove helpful to you.

I have tried to provide the scripture texts for each sermon prior to (or within) the sermon. Who read the biblical text(s), and when, in relation to the sermon depended on the custom of the church or chapel when I arrived. In the same way, "local usage" explains the variety of versions employed.

More than a few of these sermons were based on the 1984 edition of the New International Version of the Bible (NIV 1984), but since that version is no longer available to be included in publications, I have substituted other versions in the book—hopefully, with minimal confusion.

๑๛

I pray that something in what follows will inspire you or intrigue you, or comfort you, or encourage or challenge you. There was no sermon in this book that God did not intend for me to hear along with the people who sat in the pews (or chairs) when I preached it. And because I spent more time with the sermons than any of those who heard them, I trust the impact was greatest upon me. And now I hope that somewhere here you will read words through which God's Spirit will speak to your faith and reveal God's purpose for it—and many other things.

๑๛

Sermons

From the Gospel of Mark

Gospel of Mark

Ephesians 2:12-18 RSV

In the Book of Ephesians, Paul is explaining the miracle of grace revealed in Jesus Christ our Redeemer. Paul explains that we who were separated from God by our sins are brought near to God, not by our working our way back to God, but by God coming close to us, in the person of Jesus Christ.

৵৽

12 …remember that you were at that time separated from Christ, alienated from the commonwealth of Israel, and strangers to the covenants of promise, having no hope and without God in the world. 13 But now in Christ Jesus you who once were far off have been brought near in the blood of Christ. 14 For he is our peace, who has made us both one, and has broken down the dividing wall of hostility, 15 by abolishing in his flesh the law of commandments and ordinances, that he might create in himself one new man in place of the two, so making peace, 16 and might reconcile us both to God in one body through the cross, thereby bringing the hostility to an end. 17 And he came and preached peace to you who were far off and peace to those who were near; 18 for through him we both have access in one Spirit to the Father.

৵৽

Mark 1:14-15 RSV

Jesus has been baptized—anointed for His ministry.

He has spent time with the Spirit in the desert, preparing for His ministry and taking on the temptations of the devil.

Now, Jesus leaves His home to launch His ministry, in fulfillment of scripture and of God's intent. And He begins by offering a simple message that will transform everyone who takes it to heart.

❧

[14] *Now after John was arrested, Jesus came into Galilee, preaching the gospel of God,* [15] *and saying, "The time is fulfilled, and the kingdom of God is at hand; repent, and believe in the gospel."*

❧

1.

Here and Now, Repent and Believe

Ephesians 2:12-18; Mark 1:14-15 RSV

It is hard to imagine the beginning of the ministry of Jesus. It's hard to imagine the way it really was. We know too much about what followed—and what follows still.

But imagine anyway, as best you can, a lone Stranger stirring up the dust of what passes for a road—or striding over a nearby hilltop from somewhere else beyond. Imagine a Stranger Who is not so strange because He wears the same kind of clothes and speaks with the same accent as everyone else—a Workman of the common sort, as evidenced by the strength of His hands and the shape of His shoulders.

And yet, when the Stranger gets close enough to speak, what He says seems both presumptuous and preposterous: *"The time has come. The kingdom of God is near. Repent and believe the good news!"*

"What kind of talk is *that*? And who do You think You are to come here and talk to me—to us—like that?"

The unknown Speaker has what we would call "a credibility problem." He lacks name recognition (for now, anyway). His talking points have not been sufficiently tested with focus groups. The message hasn't, apparently, been screened or vetted or polished up by anyone. Here's a Fellow Who just shows up out of

7

nowhere and starts spouting the most bizarre sort of stuff, without any of the kinds of preparation any good PR firm would provide a client. It's a wonder that this first day on the job wasn't His last.

But it wasn't. The Stranger just started wandering around the countryside, telling whoever He ran into that everything in the world had changed, and they needed to change, too—radically— as a result. The amazing thing is not that some of the people He talked to rejected Him. The amazing thing is that *anybody* He talked to *believed* Him. *"The time is fulfilled. The kingdom of God has come near."* And people believed Him!

In a time when every day was the same as the one before it— and the ten thousand days before that—there were people who believed Him when He came and said, "This is a new time, unlike any there has ever been in all of history. As of today, you are now living in and experiencing the time toward which all of history has been moving. *The time is fulfilled.*"

❧

"And the kingdom of God has come near."
You could look around—make a 360-degree circle—and see the exact same scene you always saw. If a divine kingdom has moved into the old neighborhood, there's certainly no sign of it: no palace—no parade ground—no glorious metropolis, teeming with the trappings of power.

But this Stranger shows up and says God and the kingdom that belongs to God are as close as the tips of your fingers—or the end of your nose—or the repentance of your heart. "The kingdom of God," He says to everyone He meets, "is right here, right now."

It's preposterous!

And then He says, "Because God is right here, right now— repent. Change your mind about yourself and how you're living your life, and instead of thinking that what you've been thinking about everything is the truth, believe what I am telling you is true— about God—and about you—and about everything. Believe *Me.*"

Preposterous and presumptuous!

The message is preposterous. And to think that You have the right or authority to say this stuff to somebody—or anybody—is presumptuous in the extreme. And yet, that is how Jesus began His ministry. (And you know where it went from there.)

෩෧

But have you considered that, just as Jesus began His ministry that day, so Jesus is beginning His ministry today—again— beginning as He has every day from that first day until this?

Every day, Jesus comes as a Stranger to countless people in this world with this same preposterous and presumptuous message: "Wherever you are—whoever you are—whatever is going on in your life—and whatever you think about what is going on—the time is now, and the place is here."

The kingdom of God has come to you, and right now, you can step out of the dark and sinful world you have been living in, right into another, infinitely better world, as easily as stepping through a looking glass into a world that looks for all the world just like the one you've been living in, but that is, in fact, *God's* world, a world so wonderful and different that it will change everything you ever thought about anything.

෩෧

Now, skeptics and scoffers in our day and our world respond in the same way as their counterparts did when Jesus was a Stranger to the world and first came down the road with His call for repentance and faith—faith in what He had to say about God and us.[1]

Now, Jesus has the most famous face in the world. His name is recognized around the globe—and is probably spoken more

---

[1] Matthew 13:53-58.

9

frequently than any other (including by many who are the most resistant to His message).

Some things *have* changed since that day Jesus first came preaching. The pace of life has picked up, exponentially. Every day dawns with some new development or discovery. And it seems preposterous to suggest that "now" is the time, rather than any other—or that "time," so full of everything man can come up with, could, in any real way, be "fulfilled."

Can you believe today that the kingdom of God is as close as your breath when you have breathed it out (or breathed it in)?

Today, the skeptic is certain that there is no spiritual kingdom—here or anywhere—because he is sure there is no God. Any talk of God is preposterous to "the modern mind" and anyone who would talk of God—or for God—is considered presumptuous, and should be prevented from speaking, if possible, and punished in some way, if he does speak.

The call to repentance is taken as an insult to "good people," and the invitation to faith in the gospel of Jesus Christ as the means to enter into this supernatural kingdom is seen as almost certainly an indication of mental deficiency on the part of "the inviter."

And yet, Jesus still comes preaching the good news about God. And people continue to hear what He says and repent of their sins and of their hard and hostile attitudes, and believe, against all odds and all skeptical logic, in the good news Jesus preaches.

And people continue to discover, despite all skeptical assurances to the contrary, that there is a kingdom of God, and that it is so near that anyone who will repent and believe can enter it. Those who hear the gospel and take their chances on this kingdom of God that Jesus talked (and keeps talking) about understand that the message of Jesus is only preposterous if it is not true. And having found His message to be true, we who believe now know that it is all the ridicule and criticism of the skeptics that is preposterous.

And announcing the coming of God's kingdom—and calling for people to repent of their present lives and come into God's now-available kingdom through faith—is only presumptuous if the speaker has no authority to speak (or no power to back it up). It is no presumption for a commanding officer to call his subordinates to fall into ranks and come to attention, nor for the adjutant, much junior in rank, to call out the same command to the company or battalion, for the adjutant speaks with the delegated authority of the commander himself. And so Jesus came preaching, first in the guise of the lowly adjutant, and since Easter, in the divine revelation of His own commanding authority.

How could Jesus presume to say something so seemingly preposterous? Jesus could say what He said about the kingdom of God coming near because the kingdom had come *in Him*.

Wherever He went—wherever He was—*there* was the kingdom of God. When nothing in the world seemed different—everything in the world *was* different—because *He* was in the world, making it different.

And today, as Jesus comes preaching the good news of God in a world where everything is always different, He is still in the world through His Spirit, and still making His message true—even though He speaks the timeless message in our modern languages—speaking though us who believe, in fact—through *our* words and *our* actions on His behalf.

And what we say about the kingdom is anything but preposterous—and our speaking is anything but presumptuous—because Jesus the Christ is in this world and in us as we speak His words to this world. We are the adjutants of the King Who rules the kingdom that has been brought near enough for any sinner to enter into it.

Today, for someone, the time is fulfilled. For someone—perhaps many "someones"—the kingdom of God is here, present, available—open to every "someone" who will repent and believe the good news. It sounds preposterous, but it's the truest thing in the world. Jesus was presumptuous enough to tell you so—and so are we who have already repented and believed and entered His kingdom—the kingdom He has now brought near for you.

2.

The Gospel's Five "Ws"[2]

Mark 1:14-15 NRSV

[14] Now after John was arrested, Jesus came to Galilee, proclaiming the good news of God, [15] and saying, "The time is fulfilled, and the kingdom of God has come near; repent, and believe in the good news."

৵৽

The four Gospels—Matthew, Mark, Luke and John—are, like all of scripture, inspired by God.[3] But each of them bears a unique imprint and reflects the particular personality of its human author. Matthew seems to be something of a historian, footnoting the life of Jesus with the Old Testament promises He fulfills. Luke has the heart of a novelist, presenting Jesus in vivid and gripping scenes, and preserving the most moving stories that Jesus Himself told. John comes to the task with the mind of a philosopher, plumbing the depths of meaning, and tying the many details of Jesus to a single theme.

---

[2] As indicated in the Preface, this is the second of three sermons based on Mark 1:14-15 in the book. The sermon that follows on page 17 will be an expanded, (but still very similar) "development" of this one. This version—more of a homily than a sermon—was prepared for a communion service in a multiple-service setting with significant time constraints.

[3] 2 Timothy 3:16.

Mark, on the other hand, is more like a journalist, getting the news out to the public and cutting to the chase: "Who—what—when—where—and why."

The "Who" is Jesus. *Jesus* came preaching. To the eye-witnesses, Jesus had to be just an average-looking guy telling people something so incredible that it's incredible anybody believed Him.

"Oh, but it's Jesus, the Son of God."

But *they* didn't know that. It was just a guy from down the road showing up one day and saying what sounded for all the world like madness.

Only it wasn't madness, any more than Jesus was an ordinary individual. What it was, was the gospel of God—a bit of good news almost, but not quite, beyond belief: *"The time is fulfilled. The kingdom of God is at hand."*

The time is fulfilled: All of history—all of life as we know it—has been preparing for this. Everything then and now is part of God's getting the world ready for Jesus to come preaching the gospel.

The kingdom of God is at hand: Deliverance is at your fingertips. Grace and glory are within your grasp—if you will let go of what you're holding on to and hold on to God instead.

And that is the remarkably, breathtakingly simple gospel of God. That's the "what" our journalistic Gospel writer is so keen to convey to his readers.

And there's a "when"—the historical context: *"After John was arrested, Jesus came…preaching the gospel of God."* What a disaster the arrest of John the Baptist was! God-fearing, God-loving people were stunned, horrified and grief-stricken. They felt defeated and disheartened. And yet, after this terrible thing happened, Jesus came preaching the gospel—the good news—of God.

There is always a historical context when Jesus comes preaching. After you lose a loved one—after you have a stroke or get diagnosed with cancer—after your marriage breaks up or your kid gets in trouble—after your candidate loses or your retirement fund evaporates—after the greatest disappointments and catastrophes in your life—Jesus comes preaching the gospel of God.

When your world is falling apart, Jesus comes preaching. Perhaps because your world *is* falling apart—Jesus comes preaching. He comes preaching the good news of God: hope—redemption—salvation—a new life—a new future—a new relationship with God Himself.

Jesus came preaching in Galilee. He came to a concrete place with real and specific people. He turned up occasionally in synagogues and told them what their scriptures meant. But He came more often to homes and shops—to places where people were living their lives, doing what people do. Jesus came into Galilee just like He comes into Moore County. He preached the gospel of God in Cana and Capernaum, just like He does in Pinehurst and Whispering Pines, in Southern Pines and Seven Lakes.[4] Wherever people are—wherever you are—Jesus comes preaching.

That's Mark's "who—what—when—and where." Jesus (Man and God) came preaching the gospel *(the time is fulfilled; the kingdom...is at hand)* after John the Baptist was arrested (a major setback in the lives of God-fearing people), in Galilee, a place where people, like people everywhere else, were living their lives.

But that still leaves the "why." Mark doesn't include it, but you know the answer. Why did Jesus come preaching the gospel of God? Because *God so loved the world, He gave His only begotten Son that whosoever believes in Him will not perish but have everlasting life.*[5]

That about covers it, except for the need to *repent, and believe in the gospel.*

৯৽৶

---

[4] These are all villages in Moore County, North Carolina.
[5] John 3:16, KJV.

15

3.

Jesus Came...Preaching[6]

Mark 1:14-15 NRSV

[14] Now after John was arrested, Jesus came to Galilee, proclaiming the good news of God, [15] and saying, "The time is fulfilled, and the kingdom of God has come near; repent, and believe in the good news."

⇜⇝

The process that marked the greatest change in the history of the world began with amazing simplicity: Jesus came preaching the gospel of God. A new American administration began this week[7] with solemn ceremonies and joyous celebrations. There was a long parade, and parties lasting throughout the night. Millions of people took part directly, and hundreds of millions watched around the world.

By contrast, the salvation of the world began with one Man walking, alone, a few miles down the road to tell people who never saw Him before that the kingdom of God had come because *He* had come. To the eyewitnesses, He was surely just an average-

---

[6] The title of this sermon was chosen as a subtle tribute to Dr. George Buttrick, one of my professors in preaching, whose Lyman Beecher Lectures on preaching, published in 1931, bore this same title.

[7] The sermon was first preached on January 25, 2009.

17

looking fellow telling people something so incredible that it's incredible anybody ever believed Him.

"Oh, but it was Jesus! The Son of God was entering our world and our lives—sharing our experience. God was coming to us in Jesus."

Yes, but *they* didn't know that. It was just a guy from down the road showing up one day and saying stuff that sounded for all the world like madness.

But it wasn't madness, any more than Jesus was an ordinary man. What it was was the gospel of God—a bit of good news almost, but not quite, beyond belief: *"The time is fulfilled. The kingdom of God is at hand."*

What is He saying?

All of history—all of life as we know it—has been preparing for this. Everything then and now is part of God's getting the world ready for Jesus to come preaching the gospel.

But it is amazing to imagine: The salvation of the world was made dependent on one Man telling other people that God was turning their world upside down. It's amazing, but His purpose was not to amaze; it was to inform. Jesus did not coerce. He did not manipulate or intimidate. He instructed and then invited men and women to freely respond to the new information He provided them. He preached, and the result was totally dependent on personal, voluntary response.

Paul says *"...it pleased God by the foolishness of preaching to save them that believe."* [8] What Jesus was doing, according to Paul, was foolishness. Preaching is foolish in the sense that there is no guarantee of success in preaching—no certainty of positive response.

And success depends on response. Without the hearer's response, truth—even essential, ultimate truth—is irrelevant. It is idle power—ready, able, but untapped.

---

[8] 1 Corinthians 1:21, KJV.

Now Jesus had power. He came preaching, but He also came performing miracles[9]—healing the sick[10]—feeding multitudes.[11] But that was later. And it wasn't why He came. He came preaching—telling. The miracles were merely illustrations of the message He was delivering. What He did was done to demonstrate that the message He preached was true.

You could also make a case for the foolishness of preaching in His choice of audience. Jesus preached not to the high and mighty—except when they forced Him to.[12] He preached to the poor and lowly, the down and out, the last people in the social structure with any clout or capability to make His message a success.[13]

Jesus came preaching. And, according to the Gospel of John, *"to all who received Him,* [whoever they were] *...He gave power to become children of God."*[14] That's because when Jesus came preaching, God entered our world, our lives and our human experience in a way He had never done before. God came to us when we did not deserve it and could not go to Him.[15] God came to us when He had no obligation to do so and every reason not to.[16] Yet when Jesus came preaching, it was God speaking in the tones and terms of man.

There was also a historical context to this preaching: *"Jesus came preaching,"* according to Mark, *"after John was arrested."* What a disaster the arrest of John the Baptist was for the God-fearing, God-loving people! When they arrested John the Baptist, people were stunned, horrified, grief-stricken.

---

9 Matthew 14:22-33; John 2:1-11.
10 Mark 6:54-56.
11 Mark 6:41-44.
12 Matthew 26:63-64; John 18:33-37.
13 Matthew 11:5; Luke 4:18.
14 John 1:12, RSV.
15 Romans 5:6-8.
16 Romans 5:10.

They were mad as—well, they were extremely mad—seemingly defeated and certainly disheartened. And after this terrible thing happened, *Jesus came preaching* the gospel—the good news—of God.

๑๛

That was the historical context when Jesus came preaching—the first time. There is always a historical context when Jesus comes preaching. After you lose a loved one—after you have a stroke or get diagnosed with cancer—after your marriage breaks up or your kid gets in trouble—after your candidate loses or your retirement fund evaporates—after the greatest disappointments and catastrophes in your life—Jesus comes preaching the gospel of God.

When your world is falling apart, Jesus comes preaching. Perhaps because your world *is* falling apart—or seems so to you—Jesus comes preaching. He comes preaching the good news of God: hope—redemption—salvation—a new life—a new future—a new relationship with God Himself.

After John was arrested, Jesus came preaching. And He continued to come preaching, day after day, throughout His earthly ministry, and then *beyond* His earthly ministry. When Peter stood up to speak on Pentecost and Paul addressed the crowds in Athens, it was Jesus Who came preaching. When Billy Sunday[17] or Billy Graham, or whoever you like, delivered a sermon, Jesus came preaching. When I and all the other preachers step into the pulpit, Jesus comes preaching. When *you* speak a word of Christian witness to another, Jesus comes preaching—proclaiming with power the gospel of God—in your humble and perhaps halting words.

---

[17] Billy Sunday was a major league baseball player in the 1880s who later became the most famous preacher in American during the first 20 years of the 20th century.

Jesus came preaching in a concrete time—and a concrete place: *"After John was arrested, Jesus came into Galilee preaching…"* And in the same way Jesus came into Galilee, He comes here. He preached the gospel of God in Cana and Capernaum, just like He does in our town and the next one over and the one beyond that. Wherever people are—wherever *you* are—Jesus comes preaching.

Oh, sometimes He shows up in a worship service. He turned up in a few synagogues[18] and told them what their scriptures meant.[19]

But He came more often to homes and shops—to places where people were going about their business, living their lives, doing what people do. Jesus comes to each of us, preaching the gospel of God.

There you are, sitting around the kitchen table, reading the paper or paying your bills—or lying awake at night wondering what you're going to do about this problem or that. You're out filling your day with whatever you fill it with—and Jesus comes preaching the gospel of God. Jesus comes preaching, first to you, and then— if you believe the gospel—and sometimes even if you don't—He preaches the gospel through you to others who may yet come to believe it.

❧

Perhaps we should talk a little about this gospel of God Jesus came—and still comes—preaching. The gospel of God is remarkably, breathtakingly simple: *"The time is fulfilled. The kingdom of God is at hand. Repent and believe."*

It boggles the mind. It's almost too hard to believe, in this modern age when we know so much and believe so little. But is it any harder to believe now than it was the first time Jesus came preaching this gospel of God—when there was no track record of

---

[18] Mark 1:21, 39; 3:1; 6:2.
[19] Luke 4:16-21.

faith rewarded, or belief in the gospel proven with signs and wonders and the indwelling presence of the Holy Spirit?

Unbelievable! And yet, people believed.

Why? And how?

They let their desire win out over their doubt. They wanted the gospel to be true so much that they were willing to believe that it *was* true, simply on the word of this Man Who came to them, telling them it was.

They repented of whatever they needed to repent of, and they believed the gospel—believed that what Jesus told them was true—so true that it was the ultimate truth about everything. And they discovered, by believing, that it *was* true. And Jesus has built His church, preaching the gospel to people who decide to believe and find it just as He said it was.

Jesus came preaching—preaching the unbelievable message we *must* believe: *The time is fulfilled.* Heaven is here. *The kingdom of God is at hand.* Deliverance is at your fingertips. Grace and glory are within your grasp—if you will let go of what you're holding on to and hold on to God instead.

"The time is fulfilled. The kingdom of God is at hand. Repent and believe."

Repent: Turn away from—turn around—reject the current way, behavior, attitude and perspective. Let go of the wrong things you're grasping, the things you're holding onto for dear life, and hold onto God and His gospel for dear life instead. Let go of *this* life—*this* world—*this* idea of reality that colors your thoughts and controls your actions. And embrace the life God gives, and the eternity He gives.

And believe: Receive the message. Accept the idea that there is a reality other than the one the world embraces and promotes. Reach out and touch it. Open your hand and your heart and receive it as a free gift. Live according to a new and very different structure of things.

That's what Jesus came preaching. And, of course, anybody with any sense will tell you, it's all nonsense—foolishness. The world knows better today. We've outgrown all this supernatural stuff.

And yet....

Jesus still comes preaching the gospel of God and calling people to repentance and faith. And people are still responding in repentance and faith and finding the impossible to be possible and the incredible to be very, very believable. And the other structure—the other reality—He says is there is really *there*.

What will you do with the gospel Jesus came—and still comes—preaching? You have to do something with it. You have to accept it or reject it. You have to believe it—or not. Jesus came preaching, calling you to cast your vote for faith and against the other candidate: doubt. Cast your vote for God and you will inaugurate not a new administration, but an eternal relationship with Him.

It's that simple.

Jesus says so.

ॐॐ

Mark 1:21-28 NRSV

[21] They went to Capernaum; and when the sabbath came, [Jesus] entered the synagogue and taught. [22] They were astounded at his teaching, for he taught them as one having authority, and not as the scribes. [23] Just then there was in their synagogue a man with an unclean spirit, [24] and he cried out, "What have you to do with us, Jesus of Nazareth? Have you come to destroy us? I know who you are, the Holy One of God." [25] But Jesus rebuked him, saying, "Be silent, and come out of him!" [26] And the unclean spirit, convulsing him and crying with a loud voice, came out of him. [27] They were all amazed, and they kept on asking one another, "What is this? A new teaching—with authority! He commands even the unclean spirits, and they obey him." [28] At once his fame began to spread throughout the surrounding region of Galilee.

☙❧

4.

In Class with Jesus

Mark 1:21-28 NRSV

Last week, Jesus came preaching the gospel of God: "*The time is fulfilled. The kingdom of God is at hand. Repent and believe.*"

But that was the beginning of the process of salvation, not the end. What is supposed to happen after you repent and believe?

According to Mark, those who responded to the gospel, like Peter and Andrew, James and John, were immediately enrolled in school—"Jesus School." Believers became disciples—students. And Jesus became their Teacher.

In this Jesus School, where Jesus was both the Teacher and the Curriculum, there were lectures[20] and practical, hands-on demonstrations,[21] and a pop quiz from time to time.[22] They took field trips.[23] There were day and night classes.[24] They met during the week and on weekends.[25]

Early in the first term (Mark says), Jesus, with His matriculated students in tow, went to the village of Capernaum and, on the

---

[20] Matthew 5—7.
[21] Mark 1:41; 7:33.
[22] Matthew 16:13, 15.
[23] Luke 8:26; Matthew 15:21.
[24] Matthew 13:1-3; 14:15-20; John 3:1-2.
[25] John 4:1-3, 27, 31-34; Mark 6:1-2.

Sabbath, entered the synagogue and taught. Can you imagine what an interesting place that synagogue must have been when Jesus showed up and started teaching? The Bible says they were astonished by the authority with which He taught. Somebody went crazy—or got his sanity back. It's not that Jesus was teaching anything different—He said later that He came to fulfill the Law and the Prophets—the standard synagogue curriculum—not to destroy them.[26]

But when Jesus taught the Bible, things happened. Lives were changed. Hardened hearts were broken and then mended. Confused and darkened thinking was corrected as the true wisdom of God replaced the false wisdom of the world.

Of course, these things continue to occur when people study the Bible under the guidance of the Holy Spirit: The Spirit of God reveals the presence of God and unleashes the power of God.

Jesus went to the synagogue on the Sabbath, and Luke adds, *"as was His custom."* [27] This is what Jesus always did on the Sabbath—what He had been doing all His life. Where do you think He picked up the building blocks for His astonishingly authoritative teaching? Every week of His life, He gathered with His Nazareth neighbors to study God's word. As a result, Jesus knew the scriptures.

But He also knew that the designated speakers in the synagogue would surround the word of God with the opinions and advice of men. He knew that, for all their good intentions, they were obscuring the power of God's word in clouds of commentary.[28] And He knew that God wanted covenant relationship, not obsessive adherence to rigid rules—even rules about how to keep the rules of the Bible.[29] So when Jesus taught, He did not pile up a mountain of additions, exceptions and

---

[26] Matthew 5:17.
[27] Luke 4:16, NRSV.
[28] Matthew 23:1-4.
[29] Hosea 6:6.

elaborations. He unearthed the power of God in whatever passage they were reading. He taught with a unique and astonishing authority.

You would expect that—of Jesus—even if those in the synagogue didn't. But what you may not have expected is that those who sat at His feet and studied under Him and learned the lessons He taught received that same astonishing authority—from Him.[30] And then those disciples stood up to teach, and they amazed the world with the authority and power of their teaching, which was really *His* teaching conveyed with *His* authority through them.[31] Peter and John and the rest went to graduate school in the gospel with Jesus, and in three years or less, they were the faculty, fulfilling the Great Commission: going…and teaching….[32]

When Jesus came into a synagogue, He began to teach. When He comes into a church today, Jesus begins to teach. And when Jesus is teaching, you don't want to play hooky or drop out. Come closer and learn more.

Every disciple is to study Christ—and then teach His message to others. God wants you to teach others with authority, insight and sophistication[33] so that you bring His word into their lives effectively. For that, you need to study. For that, you need to sit in class with Jesus.

Now, I do not believe in guilt-tripping, but I do believe in honest, sober assessment. So here's a personal survey for you: How much do you know about Jesus, even if you are a Christian? How much do you know about the Bible and its wisdom, comfort and power? Is it enough?

How well do you understand God's plan and work, in the world and across history—and in your own life? How much opportunity are you giving Jesus to teach you all the things He

---

[30] Luke 9:1; 10:16-19.
[31] Acts 2:37-42; 8:4-17, 26-40.
[32] Matthew 28:19-20.
[33] Matthew 10:16.

wants you to know—that you need to know—that He has the authority and ability to teach you?

None of us score very high on the survey, but we still need to take it periodically. What's the point?

If you are not seriously and systematically studying the word of God and the details of our Christian faith and the history of the church, you will not be as effective as God wants you to be at the work He has for you to do.[34]

Everything else you do as a Christian—from worship to service to outreach—will be unnecessarily diminished by a self-imposed ignorance of the building blocks of our faith, if you are not studying. We all need to be in "Jesus School."

Jesus taught in the synagogues in the villages of Galilee. And now it is our turn to sit at the feet of Jesus and hear His teaching and learn the deep wisdom of His word and receive His authority so that we all can live and speak with power, in and to this world that is lost and waiting for our witness.

Jesus came to the synagogue in Capernaum—and taught them with amazing authority. Jesus comes to you for the same reason—and if you will let Him teach you, He will have the same effect in you.

෨෧

---

[34] Ezra 7:10; 2 Timothy 2:15, KJV.

5.

He Can Make You Clean

Mark 1:40-45 NRSV

⁴⁰ A leper came to [Jesus] begging him, and kneeling he said to him, "If you choose, you can make me clean." ⁴¹ Moved with pity, Jesus stretched out his hand and touched him, and said to him, "I do choose. Be made clean!" ⁴² Immediately the leprosy left him, and he was made clean. ⁴³ After sternly warning him he sent him away at once, ⁴⁴ saying to him, "See that you say nothing to anyone; but go, show yourself to the priest, and offer for your cleansing what Moses commanded, as a testimony to them." ⁴⁵ But he went out and began to proclaim it freely, and to spread the word, so that Jesus could no longer go into a town openly, but stayed out in the country; and people came to him from every quarter.

∂⚬∂

What do you do when there's nothing you can do?

What do you do when you're a leper—so ugly and offensive that you're cut off from the people you love and the life you want to live—cut off from everything you want until something happens to you that you can't do for yourself?

One fellow—one leper—decided to confront Jesus—to ignore the rules of his society that forced him to keep his distance. He decided to get close to Jesus and beg Him for the cure.

The leper says, *"If You choose, You can make me clean."* Not "well"—*"clean."* Leprosy in biblical times was any kind of skin disease that looked bad enough that people were repulsed. If you didn't look healthy, you didn't fit the mold of a spiritually pure people, so out you went—out of your home, out of your village, out of the ritually clean society.

The man has been legally designated a leper. He *may* be sick; he is certainly unclean. And he is certainly suffering. Whatever the pain or discomfort of his medical condition, you can add on the misery of his loneliness and shame—he's cut off from his people, many of whom will suspect that his leprosy is a punishment from God for some terrible sin.

But look on the bright side: when you've lost everything, you don't have much more to lose. There is a measure of freedom in desperation. And the leper is already ashamed. He doesn't have to worry about preserving his dignity. Just fall at the feet of Jesus and start begging.

"You can heal me, Jesus. Will you?" And Jesus says, "I will." Jesus reaches out to the man. Jesus reaches across the social barriers and religious taboos and touches a leper with a hand that heals him and cleanses him and qualifies him to return to the life he had lost.

The outcast commits everything to Jesus and Jesus commits the very power of God to his healing and his restoration. Jesus touches the leper to destroy his leprosy. Jesus touches the leper to make him whole again.

When Jesus touches, He transforms. Jesus touches the leper, and He touches you and me. Are we lepers? Physically, no. Morally and spiritually, absolutely—all of us.

And then there is another truth: not everyone who lives the life of a leper—an outcast—is physically sick. Not every outcast is cut off from the whole of society. For some people, it's a very personal leprosy. Some people are unclean only to a few.

Seen any lepers lately—people who are unclean, but need someone else to reach out and touch them if their condition is to change? Someone else must be willing to restore a leper to the life and relationships he or she wants and needs. Jesus was willing. Are you?

Who could you make clean, if you would? Whose isolation, estrangement, and shame could you end merely be reaching out and "saying the word"? Jesus had the power to heal physical diseases. At least, that's what the leper believed. But, of course, the leper wouldn't know for sure until he tried Jesus.

What power has Jesus given you to clean up the messed up and broken relationships in your life? You won't know, of course, until you exercise it in His Name and by His Spirit.

A leper came begging Jesus. Maybe the people who are lepers to you aren't begging you to restore them. But that doesn't mean you can't choose to reach out to them and restore them anyway.

Jesus took pity on His leper—and on us. He could, and He would, make the leper clean. He could, and He did, do the same for us. Will you do the same, when and where and for whom you can?

ॐ

Mark 2:1-12 NRSV

¹ When [Jesus] returned to Capernaum after some days, it was reported that he was at home. ² So many gathered around that there was no longer room for them, not even in front of the door; and he was speaking the word to them. ³ Then some people came, bringing to him a paralyzed man, carried by four of them. ⁴ And when they could not bring him to Jesus because of the crowd, they removed the roof above him; and after having dug through it, they let down the mat on which the paralytic lay. ⁵ When Jesus saw their faith, he said to the paralytic, "Son, your sins are forgiven." ⁶ Now some of the scribes were sitting there, questioning in their hearts, ⁷ "Why does this fellow speak in this way? It is blasphemy! Who can forgive sins but God alone?" ⁸ At once Jesus perceived in his spirit that they were discussing these questions among themselves; and he said to them, "Why do you raise such questions in your hearts? ⁹ Which is easier, to say to the paralytic, 'Your sins are forgiven,' or to say, 'Stand up and take your mat and walk'? ¹⁰ But so that you may know that the Son of Man has authority on earth to forgive sins"—he said to the paralytic— ¹¹ "I say to you, stand up, take your mat and go to your home." ¹² And he stood up, and immediately took the mat and went out before all of them; so that they were all amazed and glorified God, saying, "We have never seen anything like this!"

❧

6.

In the Picture

Mark 2:1-12 NRSV

On the banks of the Euphrates River, in a remote part of Syria, lie the ruins of the ancient city of Dura Europos. The city was destroyed by war and abandoned in the year 256 A.D. It was rediscovered in 1920, and with it, the earliest Christian church ever found. Painted on the wall of the church is the oldest known picture of Jesus in the world. It is a mural—of Jesus healing a paralyzed man.

Others would paint the picture of Jesus and the paralytic and the house crowded with people across the centuries: in the Middle Ages and the Renaissance and up to the modern day. But the Gospel writers painted it first—in words—and Mark, first of all.

Let's look at the picture. There's a lot to see, but two figures stand out in a mass of humanity. There is Jesus, Who may have been sitting, as rabbis do when they are teaching God's word.

But now, He is standing, which is what you would be doing if you saw the ceiling ripped open above your head and some helpless soul, flat on his back in a hammock or blanket or the like, being lowered down in front of you.

One Man is Power personified; the other is paralyzed and powerless. It is the ultimate contrast. The two faces are focused on each other, and everyone else is focused on the two of them. You don't need one of those little bracelets to know that everyone is wondering, "What will Jesus do?"

৯৩৬

We'll come back to that in a minute—to Jesus and the man who cannot move. But Mark has put a lot of other people in this picture, and though they do not grab your attention as Jesus does, they are all there for a reason. They are all part of the picture Mark is painting.

Somewhere in the room, and probably close to Jesus, are a group of men who look out of place, like city slickers at a tractor pull. They're a bit too polished for the peasants around them—and for Jesus, too, if the truth be known. They're professionals who've come up from the capital. They're "religion inspectors," here to see if what this Jesus has to say is "kosher."

Mark calls them scribes, and they're probably scribbling down every word that comes out of Jesus' mouth. They're not happy to be there. They're not happy with what they've heard about Him. And they're not going to be any happier when they hear what He's going to say to the poor fellow lying there in front of Him. Keep your eye on them.

৯৩৬

The rest of the room is filled with fascinated faces. It's true that nothing much happens in a little town like Capernaum, but Jesus will fascinate the sophisticated folks in Jerusalem as well, the "Big Apple" of their day. The townspeople in the picture with Jesus and the paralytic and the scribes have been properly fascinated with what Jesus has had to say, and they are going to be absolutely amazed by what He's about to do. You can see it on their faces.

And then there are the faces you cannot see. Mark paints people outside the house, wanting to get in—trying to look in— trying to just "hear" in. Imagine not having enough room for everyone to hear what Jesus has to say—to hear the word Jesus is speaking to them.

I suspect Jesus would have liked to have had the facilities to get them all inside. But it's like some of the restaurants around here: You go someplace and it's packed. You go to be fed, but you have to wait outside for who knows how long—hungry—because there's just not enough room for you.

Four of those faces you cannot see were simply not willing to be stuck outside. They considered the situation and overcame the obstacles—literally—that kept them from Jesus. If you look closely, you'll probably see parts of them—their arms most likely—sticking through the opening in the roof, lowering their friend down to Jesus. They could not walk in through the door. They could not climb in through the window. But they were going to get to Jesus!

It's quite a picture Mark has painted—full of faces—full of meaning—full of the Person and power of Jesus...and of all kinds of people who encounter Him.

❧

Let me show you another picture. This one, like the one they dug up at Dura Europos, is also painted on the wall of a church. And like the one in Mark, it is a picture of Jesus surrounded by lots of people.

This picture is a huge mural painted in the foyer of the church I belonged to in Virginia (until May of last year). The pastor told me that the faces around Jesus bear a "noticeable resemblance" to certain individuals who were active in the church when the mural was painted. It must be an interesting experience to recognize yourself in a picture with Jesus.

But, of course, that's why Mark painted his picture: so that you could see yourself in it. Do you notice a resemblance? Who do you look like in the picture Mark has painted?

Let us assume, for the moment, that Jesus is not the face you recognize as your own. (If it is, you will need to see me after the service and let me explain to you the psychological concept known as the "Messiah complex.")

So, assuming otherwise, do you see yourself in the face of this poor paralyzed wretch: needing Jesus, but thinking you'll never be able to get close enough to Him for Him to be able to forgive you or strengthen you or heal you or restore you—to put you on your feet again and give you a life worth living? If you see yourself in the paralytic, look what happens to him.

Friends help him when he can't do by himself what he desperately needs to do. He comes face to face with Jesus when it looks like there is no way that can happen. Jesus forgives his sins, without hesitation, without condition, without restriction.

Jesus gives him the power to stand up firmly on his own two feet, to bear his own burdens and to get on with his life. He was a "basket case" coming in; he's a case study in divine intervention going out.

❧

Perhaps you feel more like one of the four frustrated friends, trying to get somebody to Jesus—somebody in desperate need of the word, the touch, the attention and the power of Jesus. Look at this picture: they just won't give up. They overcome the obstacles. They rise above the barriers that seem certain to keep them and their friend from Jesus.

They combine persistence and ingenuity in the service of faith, and Jesus sees their faith and acts in response to it—for the benefit of their friend. Get your friends who need Jesus to Him, and Jesus will do the rest.

Look at the picture and then honestly at your heart. Do you resemble the scribes—there to listen, but not to learn? The scribes in the picture are there to make sure Jesus doesn't do anything or say anything to change or challenge anything they consider important. The scribes think they can call the bluff of Jesus, but it isn't bluffing when you hold the winning hand.

The scribes are paralyzed, too, as it turns out. They can't move out of their fixed ideas about Who God is and how people have to relate to God. As a result, they're stuck in their misunderstanding of what life means and what God really wants from us all.

Do you weigh the words and deeds of Jesus (or His followers), waiting for Him (or one of them) to slip up and slide, if not into blasphemy, then into heresy or hypocrisy or something else you can point a superior and accusing finger at? Do you think you know God's mind better than anyone else? Do you think you know what God will and won't do? Think again.

Remember, when the scribe is fussing, Jesus is forgiving. When the scribe is hassling, Jesus is healing. When the scribe is accusing Jesus of blasphemy against God, Jesus is accomplishing the blessed will of God. Whether Jesus is forgiving or healing, He's transforming lives. The good news is: If Jesus can put a paralytic on his feet, He can save a scribe from his cynicism and sense of superiority.

க்ஷ

Haven't seen yourself yet?

Whether you are one of those outside wanting to get in, wanting to get closer to Jesus so you can hear and understand better what He has to say—or whether you recognize yourself as one of those lucky faces who has enjoyed a spot where the words of Jesus come through clearly, and the mighty works of Jesus are plain to see—you are well positioned to witness the power of God in His Son Jesus Christ. You are in the picture and the picture conveys the power of God.

If you see yourself in the picture with Jesus, you're bound to be changed—transformed. That's what the picture of Jesus—every picture of Jesus—is about. Why do Mark (and Matthew and Luke and John and Paul and all the rest of the "word painters" in the New Testament) paint these pictures of Jesus?

Well, according to Jesus, *"so that you may know that the Son of Man"*—that Jesus, the very "picture" of His Father, the image of the invisible God[35]—*"has authority on earth to forgive sins,"* and the power to make everyone broken by sin whole.

You look in the mirror every day. You are familiar with your own face. You have a sense of what you look like. But when you see yourself in the picture with Jesus—when you see what Jesus does for you and with you, whoever you are—you will be like those in Mark's picture who are *"all amazed and glorifying God, saying, 'We have never seen anything like this!'"*

శ్రీ

---

[35] Colossians 1:15.

7.

A Little Sketch of the Kingdom

Mark 4:26-29 NRSV

²⁶ [Jesus] also said, "The kingdom of God is as if someone would scatter seed on the ground, ²⁷ and would sleep and rise night and day, and the seed would sprout and grow, he does not know how. ²⁸ The earth produces of itself, first the stalk, then the head, then the full grain in the head. ²⁹ But when the grain is ripe, at once he goes in with his sickle, because the harvest has come."

෬·෯

The Bible says that people hung around Jesus because He could heal their diseases and feed them in large numbers without hiring a caterer. They also hung around Jesus because He could paint amazing pictures with words. He painted some masterpieces like the parables of the Prodigal Son and the Good Samaritan. And then sometimes, He would just dash off little sketches like the two we heard today. I want you to look at the first of the two and think with me for a minute about what Jesus said.

In about 80 words or so, maybe a tenth of the words I will use, Jesus draws what could almost be described as a verbal comic strip. The farmer is almost a cartoon character. In the first frame, he's just scattering seed on the ground—no rhyme or reason—just throwing it out there.

In the second frame, he looks even more "unfarmerly." He goes to bed and then gets out of bed—day after day. No worries about the seed he threw out on the ground.

No plowing, tilling, fertilizing, or cultivating. He has no clue as to what's going on with the seed—and doesn't seem to want to find out.

Every frame in this strip is a surprise. The third scene shows crops actually growing from the seed he threw out there with such apparent indifference. While the man floats along through life, oblivious, the seed and the earth have combined to produce a miracle: growth.

Jesus says the earth produces "of itself." The actual word is αυτοματαψ—"*automatay.*" The growth is automatic. It's a given. And good thing, for the comic figure of a farmer who doesn't know how to sow the seed in any systematic, scientific way—doesn't understand how agriculture works—and doesn't seem to care—doesn't really seem to be a factor in the growth taking place.

And then, all of a sudden, the man comes to life again in the final frame, just like somebody rang a bell.

The haphazard sower, the AWOL cultivator, the ignorant agronomist, is now "Johnny on the agricultural spot" to harvest the crop that grew out of his seed—against all odds and the consensus of informed expectations.

Jesus has sketched a story line that isn't like anything in Israel. That's not what it's like there. And everybody knows it.

But it is what it's like in the kingdom of God, which they would not know unless Jesus told them—showed them—drew them a picture. Who would have thought?

Jesus came sowing seed, "proclaiming the good news of God." Here he comes with no apparent marketing plan—no discernable system to ensure program effectiveness or operational efficiency—just scattering seed wherever. And He doesn't seem too concerned about the result. He's just up and gone to a new place every day.

And He doesn't seem to understand the fundamentals of the religion business, at least as far as the experts are concerned. The priests and scribes and Pharisees are appalled at His failure to even do the basics required under the "spiritual agriculture" laws they have preserved and practiced for centuries.

But the joke ends up being on them: His seeds scattered so haphazardly have borne fruit. And the harvest came because it was going to come because that's what naturally happens when you sow some seeds. And for all the criticism of His behavior, Jesus is ready, able, and effective when the fruit is mature and it's time to harvest the crop.

৯৽৽

It's amazing how much wisdom and insight—how much truth—you can pack into something no bigger and no more serious (seemingly) than a comic strip.

"That's not what it's like around here!"

No, but it is what it's like someplace that you never saw and never will see unless you get the message that the scattered seeds are going to bear fruit and are going to be harvested, by the Sower nobody understands.

Full understanding?

No.

Guaranteed growth and harvest?

Absolutely!

Get the picture?

৯৽৽

Mark 5:21-43 NRSV

[21] *When Jesus had crossed again in the boat to the other side, a great crowd gathered around him; and he was by the sea.* [22] *Then one of the leaders of the synagogue named Jairus came and, when he saw him, fell at his feet* [23] *and begged him repeatedly, "My little daughter is at the point of death. Come and lay your hands on her, so that she may be made well, and live."* [24] *So he went with him.*

And a large crowd followed him and pressed in on him. [25] *Now there was a woman who had been suffering from hemorrhages for twelve years.* [26] *She had endured much under many physicians, and had spent all that she had; and she was no better, but rather grew worse.* [27] *She had heard about Jesus, and came up behind him in the crowd and touched his cloak,* [28] *for she said, "If I but touch his clothes, I will be made well."* [29] *Immediately her hemorrhage stopped; and she felt in her body that she was healed of her disease.* [30] *Immediately aware that power had gone forth from him, Jesus turned about in the crowd and said, "Who touched my clothes?"* [31] *And his disciples said to him, "You see the crowd pressing in on you; how can you say, 'Who touched me?'"* [32] *He looked all around to see who had done it.* [33] *But the woman, knowing what had happened to her, came in fear and trembling, fell down before him, and told him the whole truth.* [34] *He said to her, "Daughter, your faith has made you well; go in peace, and be healed of your disease."*

[35] *While he was still speaking, some people came from the leader's house to say, "Your daughter is dead. Why trouble the teacher any further?"* [36] *But overhearing what they said, Jesus said to the leader of the synagogue, "Do not fear, only believe."* [37] *He allowed no one to follow him except Peter, James, and John, the brother of James.*

[38] *When they came to the house of the leader of the synagogue, he saw a commotion, people weeping and wailing loudly.* [39] *When he had entered, he said to them, "Why do you make a commotion and weep? The child is not dead but sleeping."* [40] *And they laughed at him. Then he put them all outside, and took the child's father and mother and those who were with him, and went in where the child was.* [41] *He took her by the hand and said to her, "Talitha cum," which means, "Little girl, get up!"*

⁴² And immediately the girl got up and began to walk about (she was twelve years of age). At this they were overcome with amazement. ⁴³ He strictly ordered them that no one should know this, and told them to give her something to eat.

෧෧෨෧

8.

God's Purpose for Your Faith

Mark 5:21-43 NRSV

Why would Jesus stop cold in the middle of a life-saving mission to figure out who, in the crush of the crowd, had reached out and grabbed the hem of His garment? What could be so important that He would put off saving someone's life? The obvious answer is: saving someone else's life.

A sick woman had touched His robe as He passed by, just because she believed doing so would heal her of a terrible illness. And it did. And good for her. She got what she wanted for her faith effort. Now on to Jairus' house.

But no. Jesus knows what happened. He knows that she is satisfied with the outcome. But He is not willing to let the woman determine the goal of her faith or the purpose for her religious activity. Her faith "worked" for her, but Jesus means to see that she knows why it worked, and what God's purpose was in providing Jesus the power to heal her.

Otherwise, her physical healing will have been a wasted effort, however impressive her faith was in pursuing it. God's purpose is not merely to heal her body, but to save her life as well, now and forever. And because she doesn't realize this, Jesus stops—to save her life—her eternal life.

45

You can identify with the woman. You know what you want to get out of your religious activity: attending worship, taking communion, saying your prayers, listening to this homily. And if you are focused on what you want and what you expect to "get out of it," you will measure the success of your religious activities— the expressions of your faith—based on *your* sense of satisfaction that they have met *your* expectations or felt needs.

But what if God looks at it all differently? What is *God's* goal and purpose for your faith? What does *God* want to accomplish by meeting you in this place, and listening to your prayers, and feeding your soul with word and sacrament?

What has to happen in your heart and soul and mind for God to define your encounter with Him a "success"?

છે~

Jesus isn't satisfied just because the woman is satisfied—that she has gotten what she came for. Jesus won't let her go on her way until He is sure she has gotten what *He* came for. Jairus' daughter isn't the only dead person Jesus will bring back to life today. Here is another. And Jesus is simply unwilling for this woman to slip back into the anonymous crowd with just a physical healing to show for her faith—as wonderful and miraculous as that healing is.

What's His point?

If you're going to exercise enough faith to reach out to Jesus, get the *full* miracle—get *all* the power—get a new relationship built on redemption—get genuine peace with God—get new and eternal life. Physical illnesses are not the only thing—or even the most important thing—Jesus heals. Healing our bodies is just God's way of suggesting to us that He can and will heal our souls, which is much more important in the grand scheme of things. God invites us to make that spiritual healing—that resurrection from the dead—our goal for our faith, as it is His.

છે~

…which brings us back to Jairus. While Jesus is holding class on faith with this unnamed woman, Jairus' daughter dies. It is enough to destroy a father's faith, even a dedicated religious father like Jairus.

If only Jesus had gone straight to the house. If only…

But what is the purpose of having faith now? Can faith raise the dead? No. Not any more than touching the hem of a robe can heal a sick and desperate woman.

But God can raise the dead. He can heal the sick and raise the dead and do whatever else it is His will to do.

And God's purpose for faith—*our* faith—is that we believe He can do all these things. God in Christ has all power—the power even to raise the dead. But if the power is God's, what part does faith—our faith—play?

Faith is like the light switch in your house that neither produces nor possesses power of its own, but by its placement determines whether the power is allowed to flow where it is needed. Faith completes the circuit in our relationship with God that He has chosen to use to convey His life-saving, life-raising, life-transforming power.

"Your daughter is dead, Jairus—don't bother Jesus. Turn your faith off."

But Jesus says, "Don't be afraid. Only believe. Turn your faith on and watch what the power of God surging through it can do." Turn your faith on and see what God will do. That's His purpose for your faith.

৯৹৯

Mark 6:1-13 NRSV

¹ *[Jesus] left that place and came to his hometown, and his disciples followed him.* ² *On the sabbath he began to teach in the synagogue, and many who heard him were astounded. They said, "Where did this man get all this? What is this wisdom that has been given to him? What deeds of power are being done by his hands!* ³ *Is not this the carpenter, the son of Mary and brother of James and Joses and Judas and Simon, and are not his sisters here with us?" And they took offense at him.* ⁴ *Then Jesus said to them, "Prophets are not without honor, except in their hometown, and among their own kin, and in their own house."* ⁵ *And he could do no deed of power there, except that he laid his hands on a few sick people and cured them.* ⁶ *And he was amazed at their unbelief.*

Then he went about among the villages teaching. ⁷ *He called the twelve and began to send them out two by two, and gave them authority over the unclean spirits.* ⁸ *He ordered them to take nothing for their journey except a staff; no bread, no bag, no money in their belts;* ⁹ *but to wear sandals and not to put on two tunics.* ¹⁰ *He said to them, "Wherever you enter a house, stay there until you leave the place.* ¹¹ *If any place will not welcome you and they refuse to hear you, as you leave, shake off the dust that is on your feet as a testimony against them."* ¹² *So they went out and proclaimed that all should repent.* ¹³ *They cast out many demons, and anointed with oil many who were sick and cured them.*

☙❧

9.

When Your Country Takes Offense

Mark 6:1-13 NRSV

Yesterday was the Fourth of July, the grand holiday celebrating American Independence. The preponderance of red, white and blue in our choice of clothing today suggests that we are still in a patriotic frame of mind.

Last Wednesday night, many of us packed our Chapel Hall and sang patriotic songs with words like, "This is my country,"[36] and "God bless America, land that I love."[37] We are a patriotic bunch. We love our country.

According to the Bible, Jesus loved His country, too. Can we call Him "patriotic"? A form of that word "patriotic" turns up in the Gospel passage we heard this morning. When it says that Jesus "came to His hometown," the word translated "hometown" is, in the original Greek, πατριδα, *"patrida."* It literally means: one's "native place." Older translations like the Revised Standard Version and the King James render it as "country."

The same word turns up later in the passage, but here, because Jesus has apparently come back to Nazareth, the little village where

---

[36] "This is My Country," Don Raye and Al Jacobs, 1940.
[37] "God Bless America," Irvin Berlin, 1918 (revised, 1938).

He grew up and where his relatives still live, it is appropriate to call His *"patrida"*—His native place—His "hometown."

On the Sabbath, He goes into His hometown synagogue. How many hundreds of times had Jesus been in that simple stone building growing up? All the familiar sights and smells from childhood…. Here's where He was brought to worship and study God's word. Jesus knows every inch of this place—and every face in it—by heart.

But Jesus isn't a child anymore. He has not come to sit with the other village boys and squirm through a worship service or nod off during the discussion of the scripture. He has come back to Nazareth as a powerful religious leader—a respected Rabbi with disciples in tow. He has come into the synagogue to teach people who have known Him all His life things they have never known. There He is: Jesus of Nazareth—in Nazareth.

And all His childhood friends and neighbors and relatives are astounded by what He has to say. They are impressed by His wisdom and the reports of His powerful deeds.

But the face is just too familiar. Childhood memories of this neighborhood Boy living a normal life are too strong, and these several hundred natives of Nazareth cannot accept that Jesus is something other—something more—than what they have always thought Him to be.

And they take offense that He would present Himself to them as something else. They cannot accept it. They are invited to walk with Jesus the Messiah and they stumble over their preconceived ideas. To them, He is and can only be "Mary's boy." And so they turn away from the path of faith. The community that reared Jesus rejects Him.

His hometown, His native place, His *"patrida"* rejects Him, and Jesus responds by noting that *"prophets are not without honor, except in their 'patridi,'"* their native places. And here, we may interpret that word as "hometown"—or as something larger.

Here, the "native place" may rightly be His "country," for Jesus will go elsewhere with the good news of God's salvation—throughout His native region of Galilee and beyond—all the way to the capital city of Jerusalem. And wherever Jesus goes with the gospel, people who have grown up with the scriptures He is fulfilling—in their hearing and before their eyes—will take offense at Him.

It is an amazing demonstration of disbelief, and Jesus *is* amazed. His "*patrida*," His hometown and His whole country, have taken offense at Him and rejected Him. What do you do when your country and everyone in it seems to be taking offense at you?

It is a worthy question for us to ask today, for our hometowns, our local communities—our whole country—all these seem to be taking offense at Christians and Christianity to an ever-increasing degree.

As our Leader experienced the opposition and hostility of His "*patrida*," so we, His followers, seem to be experiencing a growing opposition and hostility from ours. Troubling signs abound that though we love our country, our country, increasingly, does not love us.

Basic, traditional symbols and expressions of our faith are frowned upon in public settings as socially inappropriate. And, in more and more cases, they are being prohibited by law. Sharing the good news of God's love and redemption with others is now defined as rude and intrusive, and viewed with distain—activity beneath the dignity of the decent sort.

Merely advocating a biblically-based system of morality for the country is strenuously condemned as hateful, hypocritical and intolerant, while the proponents and personifications of all manner of degenerate and damaging behavior are revered for their "courage" in throwing off the prudish restrictions of the past. The Church that was respected in the past is ridiculed in the present—and will likely be restricted more and more in the future.

This is our country. This is the land that we love. But today, there is the sense that it no longer loves us or our Jesus as it once did. Yes, there is much to criticize in American Christianity—appropriately criticize. We Christians are sinful people—sinful like all our neighbors—except that we have embraced a freely-given grace beyond our just deserts.

But our Christ is not sinful, nor is the gospel we proclaim to the world—to the people at the various levels of what we consider our *"patrida"*—our native place. And yet many are offended, not ultimately by our individual or even our corporate shortcomings as Christians and the Church—but by this gospel of Jesus itself. They are offended by us because they are offended by Him.

So what do you do when your *"patrida"*—your community—your country—takes offense?

You do what Jesus wants you to do—what Jesus did and what He told His disciples to do.

You *don't* do what you *feel* like doing. You don't do what you want to do most when your country takes offense at you, which is to get offended right back.

That's not to say you don't want to: Oh, the reverie of righteous indignation! Oh, the pleasure of a persecution complex! Oh, the emotional and psychological satisfaction of complaining about those who criticize the Church, of ridiculing those who ridicule Christianity! That may be what you want to do, but don't go there.

Jesus understands how you feel and what you're going through. That's why He says, *"Blessed are you when people insult you, persecute you and falsely say all kinds of evil against you because of me. ...in the same way they persecuted the prophets who were before you."*[38] But Jesus also said, *"turn...the other cheek,"*[39] and Paul warns, *"Do not repay anyone evil for*

---

[38] Matthew 5:11-12, NIV.
[39] Matthew 5:39, NIV.

evil. …overcome evil with good."[40] In other words, do not allow yourself to be tempted into throwing mud at those who throw mud at you.

This does not mean that you hoist the white flag, roll over and play dead.

Paul says, *"Do not let what you know is good be spoken of as evil."*[41] You contend—strongly—with the ideas and attitudes and actions of those who take offense at Jesus and at the Church because of Him. But you do so in the manner and in the spirit of Jesus dealing with the opposition of His family, neighbors and countrymen.

Amazed at their unbelief—disappointed that their opposition closed their doors and hearts to the miraculous power He offered—Jesus left His *"patrida"*—His hometown—and took His teaching to those places where people would listen. He sent His disciples out into other parts of the country to teach people what He had taught them. When His country and countrymen took offense, He kept on doing what God sent Him to do. And so must we.

If our neighbors take offense, we will make new neighbors. If our countrymen take offense, we will send the gospel to other countries that are not our native place. If this generation will not hear the word of God, we will teach it to another generation that will.

Tomorrow morning, a hundred children will fill The Village Chapel for Vacation Bible School. Dozens of dedicated disciples of Jesus will teach them about God's love in Christ for them. For five days, The Village Chapel will become their village, their *"patrida."* And they will not take offense. They will grow in the grace and knowledge of Jesus Christ Who will be here with them.

As we watch our country take offense at us, we grieve because we love our country still. We love our country with the love of Christ and we mourn her growing opposition and hostility to Christianity even as He mourned over the capital of His country:

[40] Romans 12:17, 21, NIV.
[41] Romans 14:16, NIV.

"O Jerusalem, Jerusalem...how often I have longed to gather your children together, as a hen gathers her chicks under her wings, and you were not willing."[42]

Like Jesus, we will not stop loving our country because it doesn't love us. We will love it, clear-eyed and without illusion, because just as America has been the last, best hope for a sinful, broken world, so the Christ we serve and proclaim is the last, best and only hope for a sinful, broken America.

We are a patriotic bunch. We love our country. And when she takes offense at us as the followers of Christ, by His grace, we will love her all the more—for His sake and for hers.

God bless America, land that I love. Stand beside her and guide her, through [this] "night"—with [Your] Light—from above.

Amen.

෨⊸ଈ

---

[42] Matthew 23:37, NIV.

10.

Jesus School

Mark 6:30-34 NRSV

[30] *The apostles gathered around Jesus, and told him all that they had done and taught.* [31] *He said to them, "Come away to a deserted place all by yourselves and rest a while." For many were coming and going, and they had no leisure even to eat.* [32] *And they went away in the boat to a deserted place by themselves.* [33] *Now many saw them going and recognized them, and they hurried there on foot from all the towns and arrived ahead of them.* [34] *As he went ashore, he saw a great crowd; and he had compassion for them, because they were like sheep without a shepherd; and he began to teach them many things.*

ॐ

Things don't always go as planned. True for us—true even for Jesus—in *this* world. Jesus had planned a retreat for His disciples—and for Himself. It was not a golf outing—they did not bring their clubs.

It was supposed to be a day at the beach—a deserted beach: warm sand, toes in the lapping water, gentle breezes and time to relax and enjoy the scenery, the conversation and the company—uninterrupted. Great plan—but it didn't happen.

Jesus spent His life seeking and saving the lost. Today, of all days, the lost are seeking Him. Mark says a bunch of people see who Jesus and His disciples are and where they are going and take off after them, on foot, along the shoreline. Whoever they are, they beat the boat with Jesus and the disciples in it to the beach. The deserted place suddenly isn't. Now, there's a crowd of strangers where the cozy retreat was supposed to be.

The arrival of this crowd is inconvenient. The normal reaction would be irritation. Jesus responds with compassion. Jesus has compassion on these people because He sees the essential things they are lacking.

And He responds to their need. He acts on His compassion. His compassion for the lost gives them priority over His concerns for His disciples—and for His own physical and emotional needs. Those needs will have to wait.

Jesus acts on His compassion—by teaching them. Think about this: Teaching, for Jesus, is an act of compassion. He shows them how much He cares about them by teaching them. Jesus is so intent on teaching the crowd that He has to be reminded that they need some physical food, too. Jesus has been feeding them spiritually, and He will provide for their physical nourishment as well.

But first things first...

⇠⇢

These people chased after Jesus because they want to see miracles. And they *will* see them. They want to be fed—to be healed. And they will be. But first, they will be taught, because that's what they need most.

The crowd wants to see wonders. Jesus gives them words. The crowd wants to be fed. Jesus gives them seeds of the sacred to nourish their souls. The crowd wants to be healed. Jesus gives them the tonic of truth to cure the spiritual cancers they carry inside.

What Jesus teaches them will, ultimately, produce the greatest miracle of all.

His words are what miracles are made of. His words are the healing hand of God; His words are the very bread of life.[43]

Mark says that Jesus begins to teach them many things. It's not what they expected, but these people find themselves enrolled in "Jesus School." And they aren't the first class to be matriculated.

First, there were fishermen and tax collectors and political agitators—twelve in all and all hand-picked to start the student body. But soon there were others under the instruction of Jesus.

A woman in the Gospel of John told her neighbors, *"Come and see a man who told me everything I ever did."*[44] Jesus met this woman at a Samaritan well and began teaching her many things. He also met a religious leader in Jerusalem at night, one Nicodemus by name, and began teaching him many things, too.[45] Jesus taught on Matthew's mount[46] and Luke's level plain.[47] And He taught these retreat-crashers in Mark's Gospel on the beach.

Jesus *"began to teach them many things."* Here's a question: He *began* to teach them—did He get finished teaching them? Does He ever?

Earlier this month, in our Vacation Bible School, we taught 100 children for a week—five days, three hours a day.

We taught them in the fellowship hall and the choir room, in the foyer of the sanctuary and the vestry behind me, and right here in the chancel. We taught them in hallways and outside in the garden. We taught them everywhere we could, and we taught them many things. We taught them they are accepted by Jesus and protected by Jesus and saved by Jesus and forgiven by Jesus. We taught them what it means to live for Jesus. We taught them many

---

43 John 6:63, 68.
44 John 4:29, NRSV.
45 John 3:1-15.
46 Matthew 5—7.
47 Luke 6:17-49.

things, but we were only beginning to teach them what they need to know about Jesus.

For 15 hours, we planted seeds in the hope that parents and grandparents, Sunday School teachers and friends will water the seeds, and that God will give the spiritual increase of faith in their lives. Two of these children made professions of faith in Jesus as their Savior during Bible School. Many others will later, if the seeds we have planted are properly nourished.

Jesus met a hundred children here two weeks ago who were so full of energy they couldn't sit still, and He began teaching them many things.

Jesus meets people here every week—those little ones and others who have traded energy for experience, whose bodies in some cases are bent by age and illness, whose hearts are broken by grief and guilt. And when Jesus sees them, He has compassion on them and begins teaching them many things, too. Jesus meets people who have lived all their lives without knowing what the word of God means and, even then, He teaches them many things. Jesus is holding school here—Jesus School.

You see, with Jesus, the teaching never ends. "Oh, but I already know that Bible story." "I've read that passage." "I can quote that verse from memory."

But Jesus never stops teaching. The Holy Spirit never stops inspiring the scriptures.[48] Every time you go to the scriptures, even to familiar stories and passages you've read before and verses you know by heart, Jesus will still—always—begin teaching you many things—new things—deeper things—things you did not learn when you were there before—miraculous things you never imagined.

He will teach you how to be saved and how to be of service to the One Who has saved you—how to seek His face and hear His

---

[48] 2 Timothy 3:16.

voice—how to live for Him—and how to die in Him. Jesus will teach you these things—if you are in Jesus School.

Do you need to be in Jesus School? Have you learned all about Jesus that you want or need to learn? Have you learned all that Jesus can teach you? Have you learned all that Jesus wants to teach you?

Well, if you have, and you do not have anything else to learn, you certainly need to be teaching those who do. Jesus never intended that He would be the only faculty member in His school, nor that there would only be one campus in operation. He had sent His disciples out as teachers, and the purpose of their interrupted retreat was to report on the success of the satellite campuses they had established.

I am enrolled in "Jesus School."

I have learned a lot throughout my life, but I am desperate to learn more—about the Bible—about the One the Bible is about—about myself and my relationship with that One.

Do we need a "Jesus School" here at our church? Jesus thinks we do. Jesus said, *"[Teach] them to observe all things…I have commanded you."*[49] He said it in the Bible. He says it to us, here and now. Jesus wants to teach us all many things that we do not yet know. And then He wants us, as His disciples, to teach others what He has taught us.

Why?

Because the world is also teaching. The world is always teaching, and most of what it's teaching is contrary to what Jesus taught and the Bible records and God wills. The world teaches everybody it can. It teaches everywhere and every way it can. It has a school in every den and every shopping mall, on every computer and iPod.

The world is a very effective teacher. It has remarkable credibility, even though what it teaches is so often so disastrously

---

[49] Matthew 28:19, KJV.

wrong. Those who are taught by the world believe what the world teaches and always will, unless they are taught something else—God's truth—just as effectively. That's what Jesus does and what He has called—and even now equips—us to do. That's why He sets up Jesus Schools.

We will not change the world or overcome its determination to destroy itself by complaining about its descent into darkness or wringing our hands over its enthusiastic embrace of evil.

This was the way of the world when Jesus first encountered it—it is the same way of the world now. Jesus responded then by teaching many things to anyone who would listen—and by sending His disciples to do the same. Jesus is still teaching many things—He is still sending His disciples out to do the same. Jesus is still holding Jesus School. And good thing…

When this nation of prodigal sons and daughters comes to its senses some day in the moral pig-pen of its own making, it will need to know the way back to a loving, forgiving, restoring Father. It will need to be taught many things it has forgotten, truths it refuses to hear or know or accept now. But we must teach the things of Jesus now if there are to be teachers who will know what to teach when this people finally turn in their darkness and yearn again for God's light.

So do not be surprised if Jesus postpones the pleasant spiritual retreat we were so looking forward to sharing as His disciples. When Jesus sees people who do not know what they need to know, He will begin to teach them. He cares too much for them not to.

And when Jesus sees an opportunity for a Jesus School, He gives it priority over everything else we would like for Him to do.

To the disciples, the plan changed. To Jesus, the immediate plan was unexpectedly interrupted by the ultimate plan, and Jesus just wasn't going to miss the opportunity to teach them many things.

Let's not miss that opportunity, either.

❧⨾❧

Mark 6:30-44 RSV

[30] *The apostles returned to Jesus, and told him all that they had done and taught.* [31] *And he said to them, "Come away by yourselves to a lonely place, and rest a while." For many were coming and going, and they had no leisure even to eat.* [32] *And they went away in the boat to a lonely place by themselves.* [33] *Now many saw them going, and knew them, and they ran there on foot from all the towns, and got there ahead of them.* [34] *As he went ashore he saw a great throng, and he had compassion on them, because they were like sheep without a shepherd; and he began to teach them many things.* [35] *And when it grew late, his disciples came to him and said, "This is a lonely place, and the hour is now late;* [36] *send them away, to go into the country and villages round about and buy themselves something to eat."* [37] *But he answered them, "You give them something to eat." And they said to him, "Shall we go and buy two hundred denarii worth of bread, and give it to them to eat?"* [38] *And he said to them, "How many loaves have you? Go and see." And when they had found out, they said, "Five, and two fish."* [39] *Then he commanded them all to sit down by companies upon the green grass.* [40] *So they sat down in groups, by hundreds and by fifties.* [41] *And taking the five loaves and the two fish he looked up to heaven, and blessed, and broke the loaves, and gave them to the disciples to set before the people; and he divided the two fish among them all.* [42] *And they all ate and were satisfied.* [43] *And they took up twelve baskets full of broken pieces and of the fish.* [44] *And those who ate the loaves were five thousand men.*

৯০৯

11.

Like Sheep Without a Shepherd

Mark 6:30-44 RSV

I would like for us to "enter into" the story at verse 34: *"As [Jesus] went ashore, he saw a great throng, and he had compassion on them, because they were like sheep without a shepherd."*

Hampton Roads, Virginia,[50] is not, to my knowledge, a big area for sheep herding the way Galilee was (and is), but I trust you can grasp the picture without too much difficulty anyway.

"Sheep without a shepherd" conjures a disturbing image. Sheep without a shepherd are vulnerable to human and natural predators. They are frequently confused and directionless. The likelihood of them being properly fed is greatly diminished. Sheep without a shepherd are "prone to wander,"[51] and individual sheep quickly scatter from the herd and end up lost, or in distress, or both. "Sheep without a shepherd" is not a good thing. And that is how those people looked to Jesus.

Your church does not have a pastor. In that sense, at least, you are like sheep without a shepherd. I do not say this to offend you,

---

[50] This sermon was preached in a church in Hampton, Virginia, where I had been asked to "fill in" for a few Sundays.

[51] See "Come, Thou Fount of Every Blessing" (stanza 3), Robert Robinson, 1757.

or to make your experience more painful. I say this to suggest to you that Jesus looks at you just as He looked at the people who chased after Him around the lake, and He sees your congregation as He saw them: as sheep without a shepherd. What does Jesus see when He looks at your church today? You will know better than I, but I suspect He sees a fair amount of confusion and pain, frustration and maybe even anger, some guilt and probably fear about the future.[52]

Sheep without a shepherd are vulnerable. You are vulnerable right now, emotionally and spiritually, theologically and morally. There is greater risk of raw feelings, anxiety and stress. Your relationship with God will be challenged and you may question your beliefs. There is greater danger of choosing to do things that are not pleasing to God and not typical of Christian men and women, simply because you do not have a leader to protect and encourage you. Individuals are more likely to wander off from the flock, making themselves much more vulnerable than those who remain close together.

Sheep without a shepherd are directionless—easily confused and easily scattered. They are also less likely to be properly fed. You do not have a leader to guide and nourish you. This is a difficult time for you.

A famous preacher has noted that before the Christian gospel is good news, it is bad news.[53] The bad news is our human condition, and I have summarized your condition in pretty depressing terms. But the good news is what God does with our human condition. And this is a message of good news today.

Jesus looked at the people in the Bible and what He saw struck Him like seeing sheep without a shepherd. I believe He looks at you the same way—with the same reaction. And what is that reaction?

---

[52] The church had recently dismissed its pastor.
[53] Frederick Buechner, *Telling the Truth: The Gospel as Tragedy, Comedy and Fairy Tale*, Harper & Row, 1977, p. 7.

The Bible says: Jesus *"had compassion on them."* Jesus didn't have to feel compassion for those people in the Bible. They were like paparazzi; they would not go away—they would not leave Him alone—they would not give Him a moment's peace. But He did have compassion for them—because they were like sheep without a shepherd.

And He has that same compassion for you. Jesus looks upon all that has happened here, and where you are today, and He responds with compassion toward you.

What exactly does the Bible mean when it talks about Jesus having compassion? The first syllable of the word, "com," means "with," "alongside," "sharing." The rest of the word, "passion," is not merely high emotion. When the Bible talks about "passion," it means suffering. The Crucifixion, and the torture Jesus endured before it, are called His "Passion." When Jesus has compassion for you, it means He is sharing your suffering—going through what you're going through with you. Is your church going through a difficult time? Jesus is going through every bit of it with you. He "feels your pain" in a way no politician ever could, because He has already suffered and died for you. He sees you as you are this morning and His reaction is an incomparable compassion for you and your circumstances.

But that's not all.

৵৽৽

The Bible says: *"...and he had compassion on them, because they were like sheep without a shepherd; and he began to teach them many things."*

The story suggests that if you are like sheep without a shepherd, Jesus will teach you many things. What is Jesus going to teach you about what you've been going through? What *has* He been teaching you? Jesus taught the people on the shoreline *"many things,"* according to Mark, and He didn't get done quickly. There will be much for you to learn because Jesus will have much that He wants to teach you.

Jesus may teach you about pastoral leadership, and about the unity of the church. He may teach you about why you exist as a church in this place and time. He may teach you about why you are who you are as a church—why this particular group of Christians has been formed into this church.

Jesus may teach you how to be your church—instead of the church down the road or one across town. He may teach each one of you what your particular purpose is in His plan for this church and how your personal relationship with Him is going to help grow and develop and bless this church.

Jesus may teach you how to forgive—and how to repent and seek forgiveness. He may teach you how to love this church as He loves it—and as He loves you. He may teach you how to renew your hope in His presence and power among you. He may teach you how to look for Him and see His hand at work here. He may teach you how to find the "shepherd" He has chosen and prepared for you. Jesus will teach you many things because He has compassion on you.

☙❧

Because you are like sheep without a shepherd, Jesus has compassion on you and will teach you many things—and He will feed you in a miraculous way. Mark says, *"Then he commanded them all to sit down by companies upon the green grass. So they sat down in groups, by hundreds and by fifties.*

"And taking the five loaves and the two fish, he looked up to heaven, and blessed, and broke the loaves, and gave them to the disciples to set before the people; and he divided the two fish among them all. And they all ate and were satisfied."

Jesus is able to take what looks like nothing and make it everything you need. He is able to feed you when no one thinks He can. He is able to feed you in ways you cannot imagine.

Notice, though, that in order for the people in the presence of Jesus to be fed, they must all sit down together. Right now, that may be hard for you to do. There may be hurt feelings or ill will. One may disapprove of another's attitude or actions. The people Jesus fed in Mark were probably not all friends. There may have been some bad blood represented there, temporarily "on hold" because of a mutual interest in seeing and hearing Jesus. A mutual interest in Jesus can do a lot to take the steam out of a heated argument or the chill out of a cold shoulder.

They were hungry and only Jesus could satisfy that hunger. And Jesus commanded them all to sit down together. Nothing else would be acceptable to Him, and nobody who disobeyed Him was going to get fed. No exceptions. No special categories. Jesus commanded them all—and they all obeyed—and they all were fed.

What are you hungry for right now? Peace? Harmony? Understanding? Reconciliation? Hope? What is this church hungry for? Are you willing to let Jesus chose the menu for what He will feed you? Jesus may not serve up what you think you want. Jesus served up bread and fish to those people—simple but unexpected food to sustain and strengthen.

In order to feed them, Jesus looked to heaven, blessed God, and divided the food among them—in great abundance. When the people were obedient to His command and accepted their individual portion of what Jesus was providing for everybody, they all were fed and they all were satisfied.

Because they were there, they were fed. Because they were obedient, they were fed. Because they were together, they were fed—and satisfied.

As I said, Jesus didn't have to have compassion on those people. They were a nuisance—wanting a lot and offering little. Jesus didn't have to have compassion on them, but He did.

Jesus didn't have to teach them anything. They had the Law and the Prophets, and religious "talk shows" everywhere (they were called "synagogues" then). Jesus didn't have to teach them, but He did.

Jesus didn't have to feed anybody. *He* didn't invite them out there in the middle of no-where (and no food). Jesus didn't have to feed them, but He did.

Why did Jesus have compassion on these people? Why did He teach them and feed them?

He did it because they weren't really sheep without a shepherd; they only seemed and acted like it. They had a Shepherd all along— a Good Shepherd. And that Shepherd did what a Good Shepherd will do.

If you're surprised, you shouldn't be. Isaiah prophesied:

> *"Behold, the Lord GOD comes with might…*
> *He will feed his flock like a shepherd,*
> *he will gather the lambs in his arms,*
> *he will carry them in his bosom,*
> *and gently lead those that are with young."* [54]

In Ezekiel 34, God declared:

> *"Behold, I, I myself will search for my sheep, and will seek them out. As a shepherd seeks out his flock when some of his sheep have been scattered abroad, so will I seek out my sheep; and I will rescue them from all places where they have been scattered on a day of clouds and thick darkness…. I myself will be the shepherd of my sheep…says the Lord GOD."* [55]

And in John 10, Jesus Himself announces:

> *"I am the good shepherd. The good shepherd lays down his life for the sheep…. I know my own and my own know me…. [M]y sheep hear my voice, and I know them, and they follow me…."* [56]

Your church does not have a pastor, and the events of the past few months could make you all feel like sheep without a shepherd. But you are God's sheep, the people of His pasture, and the good news this morning is that Jesus sees you and He has compassion on you. He has begun teaching you many things and He will feed you—all together—until you are all satisfied.

---

[54] Isaiah 40:10-11, RSV.
[55] Ezekiel 34:11-12, 15, RSV.
[56] John 10:11, 14, 27, RSV.

Jesus, your Good Shepherd, will, in the words of Ezekiel, *"seek the lost, and…bring back the strayed…bind up the crippled, and…strengthen the weak…feed [you] in justice."*[57]

And you? Know that in this difficult time, Jesus is your Shepherd. Hear His voice and follow Him.

ॐ—ॐ

May the God of peace, who through the blood of the eternal covenant brought back from the dead our Lord Jesus, that great Shepherd of the sheep, equip you with everything good for doing his will, and may he work in us what is pleasing to him, through Jesus Christ, to whom be glory for ever and ever. Amen. [58]

ॐ—ॐ

---

[57] Ezekiel 34:16, RSV.
[58] Hebrews 13:20-21, NIV.

What Do You Have to Give?

Mark 6:30-44 RSV

[30] *The apostles returned to Jesus, and told him all that they had done and taught.* [31] *And he said to them, "Come away by yourselves to a lonely place, and rest a while." For many were coming and going, and they had no leisure even to eat.* [32] *And they went away in the boat to a lonely place by themselves.* [33] *Now many saw them going, and knew them, and they ran there on foot from all the towns, and got there ahead of them.* [34] *As he went ashore he saw a great throng, and he had compassion on them, because they were like sheep without a shepherd; and he began to teach them many things.* [35] *And when it grew late, his disciples came to him and said, "This is a lonely place, and the hour is now late;* [36] *send them away, to go into the country and villages round about and buy themselves something to eat."* [37] *But he answered them, "You give them something to eat." And they said to him, "Shall we go and buy two hundred denarii worth of bread, and give it to them to eat?"* [38] *And he said to them, "How many loaves have you? Go and see." And when they had found out, they said, "Five, and two fish."* [39] *Then he commanded them all to sit down by companies upon the green grass.* [40] *So they sat down in groups, by hundreds and by fifties.* [41] *And taking the five loaves and the two fish he looked up to heaven, and blessed, and broke the loaves, and gave them to the disciples to set before the people; and he divided the two fish among them all.* [42] *And they all ate and were satisfied.* [43] *And they took up twelve baskets full of broken pieces and of the fish.* [44] *And those who ate the loaves were five thousand men.*

૭∾૭

12.

What Do You Have to Give?

Mark 6:30-44 RSV

The passage this morning is the same one we read last time. But the sermon will be different because, as is so often the case in the Bible, there is more revelation and inspiration in this one passage than one sermon can do justice to.

Last time, I pointed out that Mark 6, 30 through 44, is about Jesus and the people—people who need Him—people who come looking for Him—people who are willing to listen to Him.

Today, I want to show you that the story is also about Jesus and His disciples—followers who are not just curious, or interested, or even impressed. The disciples of Jesus have heard His call to leave everything and have followed Him. They have responded in faith, putting their very lives under His authority.

The disciple of Jesus—the faithful follower—is not merely a devoted fan, or even a dutiful servant. Jesus calls and equips His followers to become spiritual leaders, doing what He has done in the power of the Holy Spirit He provides them. In this passage, there is an important lesson, then, for Christian leaders—disciples of the Lord.

&·&

The story of Jesus and His disciples begins with a reunion: *"The disciples returned to Jesus and told Him all that they had done and taught."*

Jesus sends them out—and then He gathers them back in: "Come away by yourselves to a place where we can be alone together, and you can rest for a while." This is the pattern of Christian discipleship: Go out into the world in the power of His Spirit to proclaim His salvation and practice His grace. Then come back to Him to celebrate the harvest God has provided and renew your strength in the fellowship He provides. Christian discipleship is both "going out" and "coming back." It is mission and renewal.

But sometimes, unexpected mission requirements intrude on well-deserved renewal time. That's what happens in Mark 6. The crowd shows up, uninvited, and Jesus postpones the Christian discipleship retreat. When He sees the people, He has compassion on them. Maybe the disciples do, too; the Bible doesn't say. Whatever they are feeling, though, a problem comes up as the sun goes down.

The compassion of Jesus led Him to begin teaching the people. The disciples watch as Jesus teaches, but the disciples do not have the spiritual vision to see that Jesus is feeding the hunger of the soul. The disciples see the shadows lengthen as the day draws to a close—in a place far from town or farm—or food. They have heard Jesus teach before and their spiritual hunger no longer competes with their physical hunger. The disciples think it's time for the spiritual to give way to the practical.

And so they offer Jesus some practical advice: *"Send these people away...to buy food for themselves."*[59] The Bible is full of folks who want to "help" God fulfill His divine purpose in a more practical or efficient way: Abraham knows an easier way to come up with a son to inherit his destiny and fulfill God's Promise.[60] The children of Israel think it will be more satisfying to have a golden calf to focus

---

[59] Mark 6:36, WE.
[60] Genesis 16-17.

their worship on than God's untouchable, invisible Presence.[61] Peter thinks Jesus ought to get any talk about suffering and crosses out of His head.[62] They are all being "practical."

And we tend to do the same thing as His disciples—His Church. We tend to draw the circle of our Christian responsibility tightly around us—and see everybody outside the circle as on his own. But Jesus erases our lines and redraws them bigger—much bigger.

"Who is my neighbor?" [63]

"Whoever needs you to be his neighbor." Jesus says.

"Am I my brother's keeper?" [64] (A question almost as old as time itself.)

If Jesus says so, you are.

And what does Jesus say when Christians suggest a practical response to a spiritual situation? *"You give them something to eat."*

Jesus is doing what God the Father sent Him to do, and He does not want to stop feeding these people spiritually for eternity, just so they can be fed physically for a few hours. The disciples need to recognize and appreciate the overarching importance of what Jesus is doing for these people.

These disciples are His assistants, called to support His work. If you are a Christian—a disciple—you are a follower of Christ. But you are also a leader of others. You are to lead the lost to Christ, and you are to lead your fellow Christians into a deeper relationship with Jesus in the Church. The disciple of Jesus is a leader. And so Jesus treats His disciples like leaders and gives them a leader's responsibility: *"You give them something to eat. You* feed them."

☙❧

---

[61] Exodus 32:1-6.
[62] Matthew 16:21-23.
[63] Luke 10:29, RSV.
[64] Genesis 4:9, RSV.

Jesus has assigned His disciples the responsibility to feed people, literally and metaphorically.

But if I may paraphrase the disciples' answer to this bombshell from Jesus, "How in the world are we going to do that?" The disciples almost certainly don't have that kind of money. There may not be enough food in that whole remote region to feed such a horde of humanity even if they could find the money to buy it.

There is an old saying attributed to the Seabees in World War II: "The difficult we do at once. The impossible takes a bit longer."[65] Jesus almost always demands the difficult of His disciples—His leaders. And He is not unwilling to require what seems absolutely impossible.

So, Jesus has given His disciples a job. And His disciples don't think they have the resources they will need to do the job. They were probably saving what little food they had for their own needs. After all, they had left their own jobs to follow Jesus. They're not earning a living when they're traveling around the countryside with Him—or for Him. Because of their devotion to Jesus, their ability to provide for themselves—and their families—is significantly curtailed. They themselves may be dependent on "the kindness of strangers"[66] for their daily bread. Maybe they don't know where their own next meal is coming from.

The disciples say to Jesus (in effect), "We don't have enough of what it takes to do the job You have assigned us."

Here's a lesson: if you don't think you're qualified to do what Jesus gives you to do, tell Him so. But Jesus doesn't ask about what they *don't* have. He asks what they *do* have—"How many loaves do you have?" And He does not assume they really know what they have because He also tells them, *"Go and see."*

---

[65] Quoted on the Seabee Memorial near the entrance to Arlington National Cemetery in Washington, DC.
[66] Part of a famous line from the play, "A Streetcar Named 'Desire'" by Tennessee Williams, 1947.

Are there resources you're not even aware you have? Go and see what you really have. Why? Because the devil is always going to try to deceive you into thinking you have far fewer resources than you actually do, so that you will be less likely to undertake the difficult, and, at times, seemingly impossible, missions God assigns.

So how do you go and see what resources are available to you? You think about it, prayerfully. You note what you do know you have. You ask other people. You search the scriptures. You imagine what knowledge, skills, and assets you might have and test them out. You grow new resources that you know you need—or will need. You usually have more within your grasp than you think.

On the other hand, you can also be tempted to overvalue your assets, to think more of yourself—and your abilities—than you should. When that happens, you can be tempted to do God's work for Him—and without Him. Don't under value your gifts, but don't over estimate them, either.

The truth is: Your resources alone are always inadequate, however much or little you have. That's why, when you're faced with an apparently impossible mission as a Christian, two things have to be considered: your resources—and the power of God. Success requires you to take the resources you have discovered, wrap them in faith, and place them in the hand of God.

What do you have that you can put into God's hand for His use? Little or much, that is where your resources—as an individual and as a church—must go if they are to support the mission of God revealed in Jesus Christ.

৯০৯

Even after the disciples conducted their fast food search—even after we conduct our "spiritual gifts inventories"—it may not seem like much. But what the disciples find they have, they give to Jesus. And they don't forget the lesson after the Resurrection.

In Acts, Chapter 3, Peter, having done his inventory of resources, tells a crippled beggar, *"Silver and gold have I none, but what I have, I give you—in the name of Jesus."* [67] And what he has is the power of God to heal the man and make him walk. What Peter *doesn't* have doesn't seem to matter much after God has used what he *does* have.

The disciples bring Jesus what little bread they discover, and what He does with it is beyond belief. We looked at the miraculous meal Jesus provided for the people last time. This time, I want you to look at something else. I want you to look at the baskets: *"And they took up twelve baskets full of broken pieces and of the fish."*

What's so important about the baskets? Well, would it surprise you to learn that there were no pockets in the clothing of the Jewish people in the time of Jesus. Historians say Jewish men carried baskets to hold food or whatever else they needed to carry with them.[68]

Mark says that Jesus broke the bread and distributed it to the people—*through* His disciples. And when everybody there had been completely satisfied—fully fed—there were 12 baskets of bread left over.

Now, what they have left over in the baskets is not the scraps from what people took and didn't feel like finishing. It's not the stuff that we would normally scrape off our plates into the garbage after we've eaten. What's in the baskets is how much more Jesus provided than what the crowd needed at the time.

After the disciples had given everybody everything they wanted, there were still 12 baskets full of pieces that Jesus had made that they didn't need to give out because nobody wanted them. Jesus filled bellies. Then He filled baskets.

Twelve baskets of perfectly good bread is a lot of food, especially when you started with just five loaves—and a hungry multitude of five thousand people. Jesus provided 12 extra baskets

[67] Acts 3:6, KJV.
[68] William Barclay, "Mark 6:35-44," *Daily Study Bible, The Gospel of Mark.*

full of food, and He probably didn't intend for any of it to be wasted.

But let's ask a question. Whose baskets are these? Where would they happen to find 12 baskets? Well, there are 12 disciples—12 particular Jewish men who are followers of Jesus and helping Him distribute the food He has multiplied—to a multitude of hungry people. Where is Jesus putting this bread as He breaks it? In all likelihood, He is filling the baskets of His disciples with it.

But don't let the miraculous meal of the moment amaze you so much that you miss the full extent of what Jesus is doing. He is also, and at the same time, setting up miraculous ministry for the future. After they give away everything He has given them— everything that Jesus has put in their baskets—the disciples discover that their baskets are still completely full—full of what became of the resources they gave Him in faith. These resources are now returned to them to sustain them and to enable them to feed others in the future. Of course, they will have to love those other people if they are to feed them. If the disciples love the people Jesus loves, they will share with them what Jesus has blessed and put in the disciples' baskets.

Jesus multiplies what we give Him beyond our greatest expectations. He always gives back what we give Him, enlarged and multiplied, whether it is a loaf or a life or a church. Together, the disciples fed a multitude. Together, they received what Jesus blessed and gave them to minister with, in His Name, in the days and years that lay before them.

What do you have that you can put into God's hand for His use? What has He put in your "baskets" today?

৯৪৩

1 Corinthians 13:1-13 ESV

¹ *If I speak in the tongues of men and of angels, but have not love, I am a noisy gong or a clanging cymbal.* ² *And if I have prophetic powers, and understand all mysteries and all knowledge, and if I have all faith, so as to remove mountains, but have not love, I am nothing.* ³ *If I give away all I have, and if I deliver up my body to be burned, but have not love, I gain nothing.*

⁴ *Love is patient and kind; love does not envy or boast; it is not arrogant* ⁵ *or rude. It does not insist on its own way; it is not irritable or resentful;* ⁶ *it does not rejoice at wrongdoing, but rejoices with the truth.* ⁷ *Love bears all things, believes all things, hopes all things, endures all things.*

⁸ *Love never ends. As for prophecies, they will pass away; as for tongues, they will cease; as for knowledge, it will pass away.* ⁹ *For we know in part and we prophesy in part,* ¹⁰ *but when the perfect comes, the partial will pass away.* ¹¹ *When I was a child, I spoke like a child, I thought like a child, I reasoned like a child. When I became a man, I gave up childish ways.* ¹² *For now we see in a mirror dimly, but then face to face. Now I know in part; then I shall know fully, even as I have been fully known.*

¹³ *So now faith, hope, and love abide, these three; but the greatest of these is love.*

శ్రీ

Mark 7:24-30 ESV

^{24} *And from there [Jesus] arose and went away to the region of Tyre and Sidon. And he entered a house and did not want anyone to know, yet he could not be hidden.* ^{25} *But immediately a woman whose little daughter had an unclean spirit heard of him and came and fell down at his feet.* ^{26} *Now the woman was a Gentile, a Syrophoenician by birth. And she begged him to cast the demon out of her daughter.* ^{27} *And he said to her, "Let the children be fed first, for it is not right to take the children's bread and throw it to the dogs."* ^{28} *But she answered him, "Yes, Lord; yet even the dogs under the table eat the children's crumbs."* ^{29} *And he said to her, "For this statement you may go your way; the demon has left your daughter."* ^{30} *And she went home and found the child lying in bed and the demon gone.*

ॐ

13.

Love—Maternal and Otherwise

1 Corinthians 13:1-13; Mark 7:24-30 ESV

We don't know her name. All we know is that she is a foreigner—from the perspective of Jesus and His disciples, that is. In fact, it is Jesus and the men around Him who are the foreigners, technically. They have crossed the border from Jewish Galilee into the Gentile areas controlled by the great port city of Tyre to the northwest.

Mark writes that she is Greek, which tells us about her language and her culture, and probably her religion. He identifies her as "a Syrophoenician woman by birth," which gives us a pretty good clue to her ethnicity and her heritage.

Mark tells us a lot more about her, of course, as he relates her encounter with Jesus. Mark tells us that she has a daughter—a little daughter—and her little one is *"possessed by an unclean spirit."* We don't know the woman's name, but there is a lot you can learn about her by watching what she does when her little child is sick.

Let's set the scene: Jesus tried to slip into town without been seen—or, at least, without being noticed or identified. He wanted a little time to rest from what had become a terribly demanding and stressful life presenting the gospel of salvation to His own countrymen, the Jews. They were following Him everywhere, all the time.

He should have been able to get a little "down time" across the border, though. He was a stranger—a foreigner—there. Nobody "across the border" should have known Who He was.

But this woman found out, and quick. She found out Who He was and where He was staying. And she had a pretty good idea what He could do. She is one sharp cookie—and determined. As soon as she identifies the Mystery Man and His entourage, she makes a beeline for His door, falls down at His feet, and begs Him to cast the demon out of her daughter.

Where's the daughter? She's not there—probably at home—but that detail doesn't matter to this woman. You can almost hear her thinking: "If You're as good as they say You are, Mr. Jesus, it won't matter where my daughter is. You can get rid of that demon that's got hold of her from wherever You are."

Here is a person who isn't concerned about her dignity, her social status, religious taboos, the language barrier—if there is one—or even if her showing up unannounced like this is a bother to Jesus. For her—this is a "whatever it takes to get the job done" situation.

But it doesn't sound like her finding Jesus and coming immediately to Jesus and humbling herself publicly before Jesus and begging Jesus for help is going to get her anywhere with Jesus. She's begging Him—on her knees (or prostrate on her face)—and all He says to her is: *"Let the children first be fed...."*

And He's not talking about *her* children. Jesus is talking about God's children—the children of Israel—the Jews—the people beyond the border of Tyre and Sidon—not people like her and her family—not her and her demon-possessed daughter.

Jesus is saying, "What I've got to give—and have been giving, freely—I'll not be giving to you"—which sounds terribly "un-Jesus-like."

But that's not all.

Jesus goes on to say, "Not only is what I have to give—in this case, divine healing—for the Jews and not for you—the reason it is not for you is that you and your people—your children—are like dogs. You aren't worthy to receive what I'm giving."

Is that what He's saying?! Has Jesus just added insult to injury? What happened to that wonderful compassion Jesus is normally so famous for?

Well, if Jesus is insulting her, this woman is not going to let that get in the way of getting from Him—from God—what she is determined to have. Can she twist the arm of Jesus until He gives her what she wants? Can she browbeat Jesus with insults of her own, right there in front of everybody, until He's so ashamed He gives her what she wants—just to get a little peace?

No, but she can match wits with Jesus. Here is a woman who has heard these harsh words so often spoken of her people by their neighbors beyond the border. And yet, "face to feet" with this one particular Jew named Jesus, this one particular Syrophoenician woman with no name thinks she has heard the hint of something else.

Has Jesus shown her the shadow of an opening in that traditional stone wall of hostility between their two peoples? For the sake of her daughter, the woman takes a mental step—or leap—into uncharted territory, ignoring the insult and acting on hope.

"Let the children be fed first," Jesus said—meaning, of course, the children of Israel.

But if they are to be fed by God *first*, she reasons, then Jesus may be saying that those who are *not* the children of Israel will also be fed by God, a possibility many Jews had not even been willing to consider. And if Jesus is repeating the common insult of comparing Gentiles to dogs because they do not comply with the Mosaic laws of purity, why has Jesus blunted the edge on the slur by modifying the usual term for "dogs" to suggest "puppies" rather than a "pack of scavengers"?

That Jesus has done this is enough for her to work with—and she comes right back without missing a beat: "Mr. Jesus, all You say may be true, and God may have sent You to be and provide the Bread of Life to feed the children of God, and God's children may be Your people across the border, and You and Your people may think of me and my people—and my tormented little girl—as not worthy to gather up the crumbs under Your tables,[69] but there are crumbs that fall from tables even when the children eat all they want, and when they do, the pets under the table are not begrudged a few morsels.

"So even by Your own logic, Mr. Jesus, You could and should spare me and my daughter a crumb—a morsel of what You have been giving so freely to so many in Your country. If You can feed five thousand with a couple of loaves of bread, can You not tear off a tiny piece of the divine power You carry with You and direct it to my little daughter—to drive out the demon driving her little mind crazy?"

And to the amazement of all the Jews who had come across the border with Him—and maybe all the Gentiles who hadn't—Jesus said to her, "Yes, I can. And because of what you just said to Me, I will. Go home to your daughter; the demon is gone."

It is an amazing thing what maternal love can do. But let's not leave it there—in the warm, rosy glow of a wonderful result wrought by this woman's deep, deep love for her defenseless child. Let's look at that love and see it for what it is—just like the Apostle Paul looked at love in his great tribute in First Corinthians 13.

The amazing thing about any love worthy of the name is not the intensity of the feeling.

Maternal love is hardwired in—it's just "there" (with a few heartbreaking exceptions). Most of us have felt it directed toward us and loved it in return.

---

[69] See "The Prayer of Humble Access" in the 1928 *Episcopal Book of Common Prayer.*

But the important thing is what this kind of love *does*—how it demonstrates itself. Yes, it's wonderful that the woman in the Gospel loved her child—and you know she did, without doubt—because of what she did.

What does love "do"? It "does" patience and kindness, especially when patience and kindness are the last things it wants to do. It shows humility and graciousness when the natural inclination is to be arrogant and rude. It does not envy or boast, even when it has very good reasons to. It does not insist on its own way when it very much wants and needs its own way.

It is not irritable, though severely provoked. It is not resentful, though unjustly treated. It takes no pleasure in the difficulties of others, however much deserved. It rejoices in the truth, no matter how personally inconvenient.

Love bears every burden placed upon it. It endures every hardship and disappointment confronting it. It continues to have faith when it cannot see any reason to, and clings doggedly to hope when so many hopes have been dashed.

Can you see this kind of love in the Syrophoenician woman? Desperate to meet her daughter's need, and yet able to show patience in her impatience and kindness when she really wants to throttle Somebody perhaps. Rebuffed—and insulted in the process—she shows neither resentment nor rudeness. She simply endures, bears up, hopes and believes—for the sake of the child she loves.

Is First Corinthians 13 just Paul's romantic recital of the wonder of love? No, if you read it carefully you will see that it is a sober assessment of the sacrifices involved in living the love of a true child of God. "This is what love is," Paul says. (And what we so often are not.)

But it is what we can be, by the grace and power of God. You see this love demonstrated in the behavior of the Syrophoenician woman even as she is contending with the very Son of God for the sake of her daughter. And you can see it in homes all over the world even today.

But it is not just maternal love that works this way. Paul is describing godly love, for *"God is love,"*[70] according to scripture, and God demonstrates His love for us, His children, in all the ways that Paul describes.

If you see the evidence of this love more in those who bear and raise children than anyone else, it only means that they have a special motivation to do the practical, difficult and demanding things that are love—for their children.

But Paul did not write this great tribute to love to celebrate any particular group of people. He wrote it for all the Christians in the church in Corinth whose love was lacking—and for Christians everywhere else, too, because they and we have always had a hard time loving others as we should, in the Church, in our homes, and in the world.

So let us not merely commend those women who have loved their children in ways that demonstrate the truth of Paul's words. Let us all take on those traits that define the love of God for us— and demonstrate His love in us for all His children.

Oh, and the unnamed Syrophoenician woman in the story? I think we know her name. Her name is "Mother."[71]

❧❧

---

[70] 1 John 4:8, RSV.
[71] This sermon was preached on Mothers' Day.

Malachi 3:10-12 ESV

[10] *Bring the full tithe into the storehouse, that there may be food in my house. And thereby put me to the test, says the* LORD *of hosts, if I will not open the windows of heaven for you and pour down for you a blessing until there is no more need.* [11] *I will rebuke the devourer for you, so that it will not destroy the fruits of your soil, and your vine in the field shall not fail to bear, says the* LORD *of hosts.* [12] *Then all nations will call you blessed, for you will be a land of delight, says the* LORD *of hosts.*

❧❧

Mark 8:1-9 ESV

[1] *In those days, when again a great crowd had gathered, and they had nothing to eat, [Jesus] called his disciples to him and said to them, [2] "I have compassion on the crowd, because they have been with me now three days and have nothing to eat. [3] And if I send them away hungry to their homes, they will faint on the way. And some of them have come from far away." [4] And his disciples answered him, "How can one feed these people with bread here in this desolate place?" [5] And he asked them, "How many loaves do you have?" They said, "Seven." [6] And he directed the crowd to sit down on the ground. And he took the seven loaves, and having given thanks, he broke them and gave them to his disciples to set before the people; and they set them before the crowd. [7] And they had a few small fish. And having blessed them, he said that these also should be set before them. [8] And they ate and were satisfied. And they took up the broken pieces left over, seven baskets full. [9] And there were about four thousand people. And he sent them away.*

෨෪

14.

Enough and More

Malachi 3:10-12; Mark 8:1-9 ESV

We come to this message from the "messenger" of God—for that is what the name "Malachi" actually means—having all but completed our annual stewardship emphasis. At the same time, we are just beginning our preparations for Thanksgiving.

Now Malachi usually gets marched out in September or October to put a little pressure on God's people to pump up the financial dimension of their faithfulness. And just the mention of the name "Malachi" can cause many of the "better informed" (biblically) to go deaf or get distracted, detecting a guilt trip coming in the guise of a sermon.

On the other hand, who doesn't like a lovely story about Jesus providing an unplanned picnic for a multitude of people who couldn't have come up with a "Happy Meal" among them? The only guilt trip Jesus gives out there in the Gospel of Mark goes to His whiney disciples who wonder how He's going to whip up enough free food to feed all the folks who came to His Bible conference out there in the countryside.

But suppose we put these two passages together and pull out some practical applications for today.

First of all, let's recall that, in both cases, the economy was a mess. Times were hard in both time periods. The Persians were taxing the one group and the Romans were taxing the other. That's why the people were holding back in Malachi and had nothing to hold back—or bring forward—in Mark.

There just didn't seem to be enough of what people needed to go around. If demand exceeds supply, you better protect your insufficient supply so you don't run out of what you know you're going to need. It seemed the only sensible thing to do, under the circumstances.

But that attitude, as prudent and sensible as it seemed, left one key factor out of the equation: God. In the words of Malachi, God extended an invitation. In the deeds of Jesus, God delivered a demonstration. In both circumstances, the audience experienced a remarkable revelation.

❧

The best efforts and intentions of a sinful humanity—left to its own devices—will always fall short in its attempt to meet the needs of people and the planet. Even the best people "blow it" because our "best" is never good enough, in and of itself. And our normal efforts—not to mention our worst—are worse. And then there are those who are bad people, by our standards—or worse.

The bottom line is that many people suffer for real—and when we see them, we are afraid we might suffer, too. The temptation is to keep what little we have carefully conserved for the rainy day we know will come—perhaps as early as tomorrow. The temptation is to cut ourselves off—morally and emotionally—from the many who need so much—from people we cannot imagine how we could help. We do not want to lose what we have that we know we need for ourselves. We do not want to suffer, either, by seeing the reality of their fear and pain and need.

So where does God come into the picture?

In Malachi, God does not address the need for greater benevolence on the part of His people. Certainly, the Bible is filled with commands and admonitions to take care of those in the society who have genuine need. But before that, God is concerned with the relationship of people with Him. That is the first and always-central relationship, and it informs and determines the economic—as well as the spiritual—dimension of our lives.

That's why Jesus would tell people, *"Where your treasure is, there will your heart be also."*[72] And "You cannot serve two masters; you cannot make material things the main thing in your life."[73] And *"Seek first the kingdom of God and His righteousness...."*[74]

And here's an interesting thing about how God engages the people He's disappointed with in Malachi.

God doesn't say, "I'm God. Give Me what I want—or else!" God can have what He wants—anything and everything He wants. "The Lord giveth and the Lord taketh away."[75] Right?

But God doesn't seem to want your "stuff"—even when He says, "Cough up a full 10 percent of what you have and drop it off at My place." That's not really the point.

❧

God is challenging people who ought to know Him better than they do, to *get* to know Him better—by putting their money—their material possessions—their materialistic perspective—where God's mouth is, so to speak. God is saying to fearful people, "You don't really understand how the world works because you don't really understand how I work—am working—in this world of yours—the world I created and control—for your benefit."

It's funny how those who don't take God (whether the reality or the idea) seriously are always accusing those who do believe in

[72] Matthew 6:21, ESV.
[73] Matthew 6:24.
[74] Matthew 6:33, ESV.
[75] Job 1:21.

God, and do take Him seriously, of not being "realistic." But who is the more realistic if reality really is what God says it is. God says that those who act in faith to enter into the supernatural relationship God offers them, in the way He requires, will have a relationship with Him that will make all of His grace and generosity available to them. And that grace and generosity will meet all the needs they know about. And then, God will supply infinitely more grace and generosity than they could ever imagine—for meeting needs that never even crossed their minds. Imagine what it's like suddenly to realize that *those* needs have been met, too.

When Christopher Columbus came back from the New World and told people what he found, many thought he was crazy—or, at least, "not realistic." The truth was that there was a reality they did not know and would not believe—real as it was and had always been. And Columbus would not "un-believe" what he had experienced just to be considered "realistic" by those who had not gone where he had.

If you will believe in God's promise and practice of grace and generosity to you by responding in kind—in faith—you will discover that you have been brought into God's new and wonderful "world." Imagine a world where the ways of this fallen, material world are surpassed and redeemed beyond imagining.

Whatever the material measure, the "reality" will be greater and richer and more joyous—as though (or because) the "windows of heaven" will be thrown open to you, and showers of blessings— God's most gracious of blessings—will be poured out upon you in your relationship with Him.

⇛∞⇝

Jesus didn't feed multitudes miraculously just because they were hungry—though He certainly had compassion on them for the material things they lacked. But notice that every time Jesus fed a crowd, He produced food they were not aware He had—food they were not aware *they* could have. Every time He fed people, there was enough for all of them to have all they wanted. And every time Jesus fed thousands with what seemed like nothing—from the world's realistic, materialistic perspective—after everybody had enough, there was always much, much more left over.

Jesus was opening the windows of heaven and showing people the miraculous reality that awaits those who will believe and respond to God's out-of-this-world, yet for-this-world, reality of grace and generosity. You can be gracious because your God is gracious in His relationship with you. You can be generous with what you have because He is infinitely more generous with what He wants to—and will—give to you when you open your heart and your life and your self to let Him and His generosity in.

So here we are, considering how we will meet the ministry needs of this church in the year ahead, and at the same time, considering how we will give proper thanks for all the blessings that have been ours in this year now drawing to a close. Is it realistic to think—to believe—that these two activities are both, in some spiritual sense, part of a deeper, divine reality?

It depends, I guess, on what you bring to God in response to His challenge, or whether you have ever had this amazing Man feed you, enough and more, when you thought, realistically, there was nothing to be had.

Experience God's grace and generosity—enough and more.

৵৽৶

Mark 8:31-38 NRSV

³¹ *Then [Jesus] began to teach them that the Son of Man must undergo great suffering, and be rejected by the elders, the chief priests, and the scribes, and be killed, and after three days rise again.* ³² *He said all this quite openly. And Peter took him aside and began to rebuke him.* ³³ *But turning and looking at his disciples, he rebuked Peter and said, "Get behind me, Satan! For you are setting your mind not on divine things but on human things."*

³⁴ *He called the crowd with his disciples, and said to them, "If any want to become my followers, let them deny themselves and take up their cross and follow me.* ³⁵ *For those who want to save their life will lose it, and those who lose their life for my sake, and for the sake of the gospel, will save it.* ³⁶ *For what will it profit them to gain the whole world and forfeit their life?* ³⁷ *Indeed, what can they give in return for their life?* ³⁸ *Those who are ashamed of me and of my words in this adulterous and sinful generation, of them the Son of Man will also be ashamed when he comes in the glory of his Father with the holy angels."*

❧❧

15.

If You Want to Follow Jesus

Mark 8:31-38 NRSV

You would think that being a disciple of Jesus Christ like Peter is would be the coolest thing: hanging out with Jesus while He's preaching the good news or performing miracles,[76] waiting for Him to make you "a fisher of men" like He promised.[77] Wherever Jesus goes, you go. Mountaintop experiences are an everyday occurrence.[78]

There you are, just sitting around the campfire with Jesus at the end of a long, busy day. You don't bother to sing "Kum By Yah"[79] because He's there already. Maybe you all sing, "I Have Decided to Follow Jesus,"[80] since you have. Gee, it's great to be a disciple and hang out with Jesus!

Or so you would think.

There you are singing around the campfire and speculating that Jesus may be the Messiah—and you don't even get the first verse

---

[76] Mark 1:29-34.

[77] Matthew 4:19.

[78] Matthew 5:1; 17:1.

[79] "Kum Ba Yah" ("Come by Here"), spiritual song first recorded in the 1920s, author unknown.

[80] "I Have Decided to Follow Jesus," arranged by William J. Reynolds, 1959, from the testimony of a convert in India in the mid-19th century.

out before Jesus interrupts the spiritual reverie with a tale of mayhem and murder. *"The Son of man,"* He says, *"must suffer many things…and be killed…."*[81]

Talk about a mood buster! Peter and the others are celebrating divine deliverance and Jesus counters with defeat and death. And discipleship is—all of a sudden—not as cool as it was just a minute before.

And it doesn't take a minute (New York or otherwise) for Peter to get in his Master's face. "Messiahs don't get murdered!" Peter tells Jesus. "The Christ isn't supposed to get treated like a criminal!"

…which shows how much Peter and the other disciples know about this particular Messiah—and about what it's going to mean to be His disciple.

"Jesus, shut up about this 'suffering and murder' talk. That's not what we've got planned for You."

Oh? *You*, the disciples of Jesus—the One you've just proclaimed the Christ—have plans for *Him?* Think again.

And just as quickly as Peter took hold of Jesus, Jesus returns the favor. Jesus "invites" Peter to "review the pecking order": The *disciple* is the *follower*. The disciple belongs *behind* his Master. And so Jesus directs Peter to his proper position.

Then Jesus "reminds" Peter of their functional relationship: the disciple (Peter) is the student; he does not teach the Teacher. Jesus points out to Peter how Peter has miscalculated the problem. Messiah Jesus—Jesus the Christ—is going to be a *suffering* Savior.

With all His power—with all His authority—with all His wisdom—with all His compassion and commitment and courage—Jesus is going to be a Messiah Who defeats God's enemies by letting those enemies defeat Him.

You can understand why the disciples are a little confused—and more than a little distressed: you think you've joined up with a

---

[81] Mark 8:31, RSV.

sure Winner, only to learn He's determined to become a sacrificial Lamb. *"The son of man will suffer many things and be rejected... and be killed..."*[82] Oh, joy!

But Jesus is not done dropping bombshells. *"If any want to become my followers, let them deny themselves and take up their cross and follow me."* And this rocket is not an intimate little insight shared with His inner circle. Jesus has opened a recruiting office and is broadcasting it to anyone within earshot. This isn't exactly the "fishers of men" speech Peter and the others got on those sunny days back on the beach. Hard to believe this cross business will draw as many followers as the images of crowns did in the early days.

Can't you just see the look on the faces of those who've already signed up. There they stand beside Jesus, popping Tums like candy and wanting to scream like the *Monty Python* characters, "Run away! Run away!"[83] Is this Jesus crazy?

No. To be honest, Jesus would prefer to run away, too. Jesus does not choose suffering; He does not desire it.[84] Jesus chooses obedience to God, and it is this obedience to God that *requires* Him to suffer.

Military conquest is what all the messiah watchers expect and desire. And who wouldn't prefer to march in triumph rather than writhe in torment? Jesus was confronted with that very option[85] and found it to be a deceitful fantasy, a temptation leading only to failure. And so He accepts the only option God provides for being a successful Messiah: the way of suffering, the way of the Cross.

"That's fine for Jesus; He's the Messiah. But what about the rest of us? Why should we have to do the self-denial and suffering thing just to be His disciples?"

---

[82] Mark 8:31, RSV.
[83] *Monty Python* was an influential British comedy group who first appeared on the BBC in 1969.
[84] Matthew 26:39.
[85] Matthew 4:8-10.

Well, I could give you a long, involved and hard to comprehend theological reason, but in the end, it's kind of like when you were a child and you asked that same question about everything you didn't like: "Why do I have to?" And your mother said, "Because I'm the Mommy and I said so. That's why."

Jesus is the Messiah and He says you have to deny yourself and take up your cross to follow Him. And that's why you have to. You can't follow Jesus without denying yourself and carrying your cross. You can't be a disciple of Jesus any other way.

Jesus wants everybody to follow Him, to benefit from His suffering and death, but He knows not everybody will. When Jesus starts talking about suffering, many of His disciples will no longer follow Him. And because of that, He asks the original twelve disciples, *"Do you also wish to go away?"* [86]

You'll be interested to know that it's Peter, properly positioned now in his place as a disciple, who says, *"Lord, to whom can we go? You have the words of eternal life."* These disciples are sticking.

And then there's you. Jesus wants you to be His disciple. If you will—if you want to follow Jesus—you have to do a couple of things.

You have to deny yourself. And to help you out, we've conveniently scheduled Lent. That's what Lent is for, right—to deny yourself something for a little while? You know: It's Lent, so deny yourself chocolate or that drink before dinner. Deny yourself meat on Fridays or, God forbid, golf. Is this "denying yourself" we're talking about about curbing your appetites a little in the cause of Christ?

No, sorry, it's much more radical than that. Jesus doesn't say, "Deny something to yourself. Do without a little." He says, "Deny your *self*. Don't even consider your personal drives, desires and motivations. Strike through every item on your personal agenda. Ignore every personal impulse. Deny everything about yourself

---

[86] John 6:67-68, NRSV.

that would naturally take control of your life and determine the choices you would make and the attitudes you would develop. Drop all that psychological apparatus at the feet of Jesus and take up your cross instead.

Fortunately, it is *your* cross that Jesus requires you to carry, not His. Jesus is carrying *His* Cross. Long before Pilate's henchmen slam that crossbeam on His bloody back in Jerusalem and shove Him along to Calvary and Crucifixion,[87] Jesus is already carrying His Cross. When He preaches His first sermon[88] and casts out His first demon[89] and takes the hand of the first poor soul who reaches out to Him,[90] Jesus is carrying the weight of the knowledge of where He is going and what He will be doing in the end. From the day He steps up out of the Jordan River and begins His ministry,[91] Jesus is carrying His Cross.

And in the same way, you must take up your cross and carry the weight of discipleship every day.

Now let's be clear about the cross Jesus has instructed you to carry as His disciple. Your cross is a symbol of your suffering, but not the normal, natural, everyday suffering that comes with drawing breath on this earth. Your cross is not the physical pain, or mental anguish or practical setbacks every person experiences in life. Your cross is what you have to put up with because you are a disciple of Jesus Christ—what you could avoid if you were not His disciple. Your cross is the symbol of your suffering *for Christ*— and of your subordination of your self in loyalty to Christ.

"But why? Why the sacrifice? Why the suffering? I want to follow Jesus, but why the self-denial—why the cross?"

---

[87] John 19:17.
[88] Mark 1:14.
[89] Luke 4:31-35.
[90] Mark 1:29-31.
[91] Mark 1:9-13.

Oh, I guess I left that part out. Jesus tells His disciples that He must undergo great suffering and be rejected and be killed—and after three days, rise again.

Paul says, *"I have been crucified with Christ and I no longer live, but Christ lives in me. The life I now live in the body, I live by faith in the Son of God, Who loved me and gave himself for me."* [92]

Jesus tells the disciple "wannabes" to deny themselves and take up their crosses and follow Him because those who want to save their lives will lose them, and those who lose their lives (in self-denial and sacrifice and suffering) for Jesus and for His gospel, will save them.

Paul again, *"...if we have been united with Him in a death like His, we shall certainly be united with Him in a resurrection like His.... But if we have died with Christ, we believe that we shall also live with Him."* [93]

If you want to follow Jesus—if you want to be His disciple—deny yourself and take up your cross and follow Him—and die with Him—and live with Him, now and forever. Discipleship: costly and—because of the Resurrection—very, very cool.

❧

---

[92] Galatians 2:20, ESV.
[93] Romans 6:5, 8, RSV.

Mark 10:2-16 NRSV

² Some Pharisees came, and to test [Jesus] they asked, "Is it lawful for a man to divorce his wife?" ³ He answered them, "What did Moses command you?" ⁴ They said, "Moses allowed a man to write a certificate of dismissal and to divorce her." ⁵ But Jesus said to them, "Because of your hardness of heart he wrote this commandment for you. ⁶ But from the beginning of creation, 'God made them male and female.' ⁷ For this reason a man shall leave his father and mother and be joined to his wife, ⁸ and the two shall become one flesh.' So they are no longer two, but one flesh. ⁹ Therefore what God has joined together, let no one separate." ¹⁰ Then in the house the disciples asked him again about this matter. ¹¹ He said to them, "Whoever divorces his wife and marries another commits adultery against her; ¹² and if she divorces her husband and marries another, she commits adultery."

¹³ People were bringing little children to him in order that he might touch them; and the disciples spoke sternly to them. ¹⁴ But when Jesus saw this, he was indignant and said to them, "Let the little children come to me; do not stop them; for it is to such as these that the kingdom of God belongs. ¹⁵ Truly I tell you, whoever does not receive the kingdom of God as a little child will never enter it." ¹⁶ And he took them up in his arms, laid his hands on them, and blessed them.

❧❦

16.

A Word for the Children

Mark 10:2-16 NRSV

Well, given the choice between talking about how much Jesus loves children and how strongly He opposes divorce—the choice Mark gives us in the Gospel reading for this morning—what preacher in his right mind would take on the business of divorce?

You talk "children" and everybody gets all sentimental, with mental pictures of sweet little girls and boys gathered around a smiling Jesus. We all love children. More and more of them are coming into our church. We want to see children grow up in the church—to believe in Jesus and live good and godly lives. "Jesus and the children" is a sure winner for any preacher.

On the other hand, nobody wants to hear about failed marriages and Jesus opposing divorce. There's a lot of pain around this subject. If you haven't divorced and remarried, someone close to you has. It seems inescapable. Preaching on the subject is a ticking bomb. People leave churches over this stuff.

Nobody's going to be happy with what Jesus has to say. Why go there?

Why go there? Because Jesus did. And maybe He did—maybe Jesus went there—as another way to show how much He loves the little children—however old they are. *You* are the little children—

single, married, divorced, widowed, remarried. You are the beloved children of God to whom God sent His Son—His unique and beloved Child—Jesus. And it is not His intention or desire that your failures in marriage—or in any other sphere of life—should stop you from coming to Him and being accepted and blessed and embraced by Him.

But Jesus will not go along with the way of the world. Though He will bless us, He will not bless our broken processes, our accommodations to our human weakness and sinfulness. He has come to inaugurate the reign of God among us, to bring the kingdom in which God's will is done on earth as it is in heaven.[94] And so, painful as it is to us, Jesus always points beyond our shortcomings to God's will for us—His children.

No matter what the world says—no matter what we say—Jesus says—because God says—"marriage."

And so we must say—as the body of Christ—as the followers of Jesus—even if we are the victims of divorce or the instigators of divorce or the acceptors of divorce—"from the beginning of Creation, God made us male and female so that we would leave our fathers and mothers and be joined together by God so that two become one in a way that no one should separate."

The world does not say "marriage" today. It says, "do not wait on God to make you 'one;' satisfy your desires without restraint or self-discipline. Make yourselves 'one.' Give no consideration to God's purpose or process. If you choose to go through a ritual—to have a wedding—concentrate on the spectacle, not on the miracle God would perform in each of you and between you."

The world says, "Make yourself happy as an individual by interacting with another in whatever way you see fit, and if you are not sufficiently happy, separate yourself from the one who has not provided you the sense of happiness you desire."

---

[94] Matthew 6:10.

And the harder one tries to be happy in relationship with another (but without God), the greater the unhappiness becomes, and the quicker it becomes unacceptable.

ॐ

Jesus is arguing with the world, and with His followers who have become so influenced by the world that they, too, have become focused on what God might allow, rather than what God has commanded.

We cannot unmake the mistakes we have made, in this area or any other, but we can point to God's way—and speak God's word—and do so all the more strongly because of our shortcomings—because we are beloved children who have been embraced and blessed by Jesus—not because we are sweet and lovable, but because we are *not*, and He loves us anyway.

Though we live in a world of divorce, we hear "marriage" from God. And we speak "marriage," God's divine plan for us from the beginning, because Jesus takes children into His embrace and hands them over to us, His church, and says, "Tell them what I have told you. Guide them in My ways. Speak to them of My love for them, revealed in what I command, not in what I allow."

Jesus speaks "marriage," not to hurt *you*, but to love *them*—to benefit those children, young and old, who may yet be convinced that the world is wrong, and Jesus is right, about marriage—and everything else.

ॐ

1 John 3:1-2, 18-19 ESV

The three letters of St. John augment the message of John's Gospel, urging members of the Christian Church, in the first generation and every generation, to grow spiritually and to beware of those who would undermine their faith.

❧◦❧

¹ See what kind of love the Father has given to us, that we should be called children of God; and so we are. The reason why the world does not know us is that it did not know him. ² Beloved, we are God's children now, and what we will be has not yet appeared; but we know that when he appears we shall be like him, because we shall see him as he is.

¹⁸ Little children, let us not love in word or talk but in deed and in truth. ¹⁹ By this we shall know that we are of the truth and reassure our heart before him. . . .

❧◦❧

Mark 10:13-16 ESV

All four of the Gospels give attention to the special concern Jesus had for children, and the great value He placed upon them. Childlike faith and innocence are prominent in His portrayal of those who will be present in God's kingdom.

❧◦❧

¹³ And they were bringing children to [Jesus] that he might touch them, and the disciples rebuked them. ¹⁴ But when Jesus saw it, he was indignant and said to them, "Let the children come to me; do not hinder them, for to such belongs the kingdom of God. ¹⁵ Truly, I say to you, whoever does not receive the kingdom of God like a child shall not enter it." ¹⁶ And he took them in his arms and blessed them, laying his hands on them.

❧◦❧

17.

Where Are You Taking Your Children?

1 John 3:1-2, 18-19; Mark 10:13-16 ESV

You've seen the bumper sticker, usually on the back of a well-used minivan: "Mom's Taxi." And if the driver had to keep a log of destinations as other "cabbies" do, hers would show an endless repetition of "school, practice, games, lessons, recitals, clubs, doctor, dentist, the library, friends, the mall—or some specific store, there or elsewhere." These days, mothers spend a lot of their lives taking their children to the places they need or want to go.

And today is "Maternal Taxi Driver Appreciation Day."

For the miles you have driven over the years—for the hours you have spent behind the wheel, navigating through traffic, keeping the peace among the passengers, loading gear of all sizes, shapes (and aromas) into and out of your "taxi," we who have called up your cab—sometimes with little or no notice and at times of extreme inconvenience—we who have ridden with you on your many human delivery missions—we who have been spared the wear and tear and lost time of driving the routes ourselves by *your* willingness to go in our place—we thank you and praise you—individually and collectively.

It is a mother's lot to be bringing her children someplace, almost all the time—which causes me to believe that on the day when an unidentified "they" were bringing children to Jesus, the "they" in question were primarily, if not exclusively, mothers. In a patriarchal society like the one in which Jesus lived, it was the responsibility of women to look after the children, just as it was their responsibility to give them birth. Fathers were supposed to love their children and enjoy them when they felt like it and punish them when they felt the children deserved it. Fathers were to name their children—giving them a public identity—and provide the food, clothing, shelter and family stability required for children to grow and become productive members of the family and the larger community.

But the women raised the children. They shared each day with them, knew each of their children intimately and did much more to mold their personalities and form their lives. When Jesus and His disciples arrived in town, the men would have come out to meet them, to get a look at Jesus and hear what He had to say. But the children would have been with the women—with their mothers.

And one day, in one unnamed village, "they" brought the children—their children—to Jesus. The scene is simple. The details few, but telling: "They" bring the children, hoping that Jesus will touch them. The disciples of Jesus rebuff their efforts and rebuke them for trying.

Jesus sees what's going on and gets angry—*angry*—not with the people bringing the children, but with His own followers who won't let those with the children fulfill their mission.

And with the help of Jesus, those who bring the children to Him do fulfill their mission. Jesus draws these children to Himself, folding them in His arms—the kind of thing a loving mother will do with her babies—and Jesus touches their children to bless them.

And then, though the Bible doesn't specifically tell us, He gives the children back to their mothers and proceeds on the mission His Heavenly Father has given Him—for those children—and for all the children of all the mothers of all the villages and towns and cities of all the world.

They brought their children to Jesus. And He touched them and blessed them.

❧

But that was a simpler time and place. Today, moms have GPS technology right on the dashboards of their taxis, or MapQuest directions on their home computers. But it may be harder than ever for mothers to bring their children to Jesus.

And why is that?

It's because Jesus is rarely to be found where moms take their kids for entertainment these days—to the movie theaters or concerts. Jesus isn't welcome on the popular TV shows or in the video games that dominate their leisure hours, or in the music children are encouraged to listen to and download. You rarely find Jesus where you take your children to buy the clothes our sexualized culture virtually requires them to wear. Jesus is surprisingly difficult to find on the sports fields and in the school classrooms and other organized activities to which your children are constantly being taken.

Of course, a mother might not want to take her children to Jesus. You wouldn't want to if your greatest goal for your children is for them to be "happy." If you take your children to Jesus, and He touches them, they will likely be in frequent conflict with the world. He was—and still is.

And do not take your children to Jesus if what you want most is for them to have high self-esteem.

Jesus doesn't care how good they feel about themselves, but about how good their relationship with God is, a relationship only Jesus can make right and rich and rewarding. With Jesus, your children won't be able to ignore or explain away their sins or blame them on "the system" or other people. They will have to honestly acknowledge their sins and confess them and repent of them in the process of being forgiven for them. There's no point taking your children to Jesus if what you want most for them is that they have every advantage in life. If you take your children to Jesus, they will be taught to live unselfishly and love sacrificially, whatever their material circumstances become.

༜⚬๑

But if you want your children to be made right with God and be saved from the condemnation they will otherwise experience for all eternity—if you want them to know the peace that passes understanding despite living in conflict with the world—if you want your children to be the people God created them to be and to live lives that are spiritually abundant whether they are materially affluent or not—the place you must take them—the only place you *can* take them—is to Jesus.

So pile those kids in Mom's taxi and take them...

Where?

Well, to church, of course—and often. And don't just drop them off. Pull that "taxi" into a parking space, turn off the meter and the engine and come in yourself. And we will help you bring your children to Jesus so that Jesus can touch them and bless them. We will not hinder you. We will help you. We will help you because we understand what it means to be touched by Jesus, to be taken up into His loving arms.

That's why we come to His communion table. That's what happens there. We bring ourselves like little children to Jesus, embracing one another as Jesus embraces us[95]—and we share the blessings with which He blesses us.

And because your children are God's children and we are God's children, we are their family. We are your loving church

---

[95] It has always been the practice at Trinity Christian Fellowship for the people, after receiving the elements of communion around the table, to put their arms around one another as the pastor blesses the group.

family, helping you bring your children to Jesus in a world doing its best to hinder you.

How old does your child have to be before you can bring him or her to Jesus? Jesus Himself was brought to God in the Temple when He was only eight days old.[96] And since God knows each of us from the moment we were conceived in our mother's womb (or before),[97] I think the moment of conception would not be too soon to start "the bringing process."

And how old is too old for your children to be brought to Jesus for Him to embrace and bless them? One Halloween, after a significant growth spurt, I went out Trick-or-Treating. At the very first house I visited, a little old lady opened the door, looked *up* at me and said disapprovingly, "Don't you think you're too old for this sort of thing?"

I was so embarrassed, I went straight home.

But no one has ever told me I was too old to be blessed and touched by Jesus. In fact, my mother brought me to Jesus in prayer every day of her life, seeking His blessing for me. I suppose she hasn't stopped bringing me to Jesus. She just has infinitely less distance to go now to get me to Him. But she started by bringing me to Jesus at church—and at home.

Imagine taking your children somewhere without having to take them anywhere. Imagine taking your children to Jesus without "the taxi" ever leaving the driveway. To take your children to Jesus, you may have to take them through the private place of your own heart—the sacred place in your life where *you* come to Jesus to be touched and blessed.

My mother brought me and my brothers and my sister to Jesus in her prayers—and in her Bible reading each day—and in the example of her commitment to the things of God year after year— and in her applying the love and will of Jesus to the practical

---

[96] Luke 2:22-24; Leviticus 12:2-8.
[97] Jeremiah 1:4-5.

problems we confronted—and sometimes caused—as we stumbled and struggled through life.

When I was a child, I thought my mother was perfect. As I got older, I got critical and changed my mind. As I've gotten older still, I've come to think I was closer to right the first time. As best she could, she brought me to Jesus and continued to do so, whatever I thought of the process, because she wanted Jesus to embrace me and bless me. And because *she* did, *He* did.

Could Jesus have done for me what He's done, if I had not been piled into Mom's taxi every Sunday and hauled off to church, or gathered into her heart and hauled up to the Lord in prayer?

Yes, Jesus has blessed countless mothers' sons—and daughters—whose mothers did not do for them what my mother did for me. But my mother wasn't taking any chances. The best way to get her children where they needed to go was to take them there herself.

Did my mother raise four saints? No, not even one. But we all were touched and blessed by Jesus because she brought us to Him.

To take your children to Jesus requires making choices, sometimes difficult and disputed choices. To take your children where Jesus can bless them means choosing to avoid taking them to other places where Jesus would not want them to be. To place your children in the loving arms of Jesus means keeping them out of the grasping clutches of those who will not bless them—who will—knowingly or unknowingly—hinder Jesus from blessing them.

Moms have to make choices about where to take their children these days. But perhaps, in this regard, it isn't really *their* choice to make. Jesus said, *"Let the…children come to Me, and do not hinder them…"* According to Him, the entries in every "Mom's taxi's" logbook should be an endless repetition of the same destination: "to Jesus, to Jesus, to Jesus, to Jesus…."

ॐॐ

Mark 10:17-31 RSV

[17] And as [Jesus] was setting out on his journey, a man ran up and knelt before him, and asked him, "Good Teacher, what must I do to inherit eternal life?" [18] And Jesus said to him, "Why do you call me good? No one is good but God alone. [19] You know the commandments: 'Do not kill, Do not commit adultery, Do not steal, Do not bear false witness, Do not defraud, Honor your father and mother.'" [20] And he said to him, "Teacher, all these I have observed from my youth." [21] And Jesus looking upon him loved him, and said to him, "You lack one thing; go, sell what you have, and give to the poor, and you will have treasure in heaven; and come, follow me." [22] At that saying his countenance fell, and he went away sorrowful; for he had great possessions.

[23] And Jesus looked around and said to his disciples, "How hard it will be for those who have riches to enter the kingdom of God!" [24] And the disciples were amazed at his words. But Jesus said to them again, "Children, how hard it is to enter the kingdom of God! [25] It is easier for a camel to go through the eye of a needle than for a rich man to enter the kingdom of God." [26] And they were exceedingly astonished, and said to him, "Then who can be saved?" [27] Jesus looked at them and said, "With men it is impossible, but not with God; for all things are possible with God." [28] Peter began to say to him, "Lo, we have left everything and followed you." [29] Jesus said, "Truly, I say to you, there is no one who has left house or brothers or sisters or mother or father or children or lands, for my sake and for the gospel, [30] who will not receive a hundredfold now in this time, houses and brothers and sisters and mothers and children and lands, with persecutions, and in the age to come eternal life. [31] But many that are first will be last, and the last first."

☙❧

18.

Give Away What's in the Way

Mark 10:17-31 RSV

Most of the strangers who come to Jesus with questions are out to trap Him. But the man with the question in Mark, Chapter 10, is himself trapped. Mark tells us he is rich. Matthew tells us he is young. Luke tells us he is a ruler. He has wealth, health, power and a proper upbringing, if his behavior is any indication.

What he does not have is an answer to the most important question in the world: *"What must I do to inherit eternal life?"* He has everything the world has to offer, but it is not enough. He is empty—unsatisfied—frustrated with a life most people would gladly trade theirs for.

But he does not have what he and we were created for. He does not have what we all want most—deep down—whether we realize it or not. He does not have eternal life. His money cannot buy it. His youth cannot win it. His power cannot command it. His morality cannot earn it.

"What must I do to get it? What must I do to get what I want most? What must I do to get what I know I must have?"

Give him credit: he's got the right question and he's asking the right person for the answer. "Jesus, how do I get eternal life?" Most people ask the wrong question. They ask questions like, "How do

I get ahead in life?" and "How can I be happy?" And they ask all the wrong people: celebrities, self-proclaimed experts, friends and co-workers—people who have no more clue than they do. It's sad, really. The wrong people do not know the right answer. The wrong questions never produce the one answer you need.

"What must I do to inherit eternal life?"

"Amass wealth," they say.

"Done that," he says, "There's got to be something more."[98]

"Exploit your youth," they say.

"Tried that," he says, "I'm still empty inside."[99]

"Exercise your authority," they say, "Flex your executive muscle."

"I did," he says, "Power's not all it's cracked up to be."[100]

"Obey the commandments," Jesus says.

"I've kept them all since childhood," the man replies, "But I know even that is not enough. There's got to be more!"[101]

"There is," says Jesus, "one more thing. You lack one thing—one thing, to inherit eternal life."

❧

And here we need to step back for a minute. We need to take stock of the situation. Ignore everybody else for the time being. Forget the crowd and the disciples. Focus on the young man in the elegant clothing, noble in bearing, even on his knees. This young man has come to the turning point in his life. Shakespeare says:

> "There is a tide in the affairs of men.
> Which, taken at the flood, leads on to fortune;
> Omitted, all the voyage of their life
> Is bound in shallows and in miseries."[102]

---

[98] Ecclesiastes 2:8, 11.
[99] Ecclesiastes 11:9.
[100] Ecclesiastes 2:9-11.
[101] Ecclesiastes 5:1-7.
[102] From *Julius Caesar*, Act 4, Scene 3, Lines 218–221.

On this day—at this moment—the young man's life has reached its flood tide, whether he realizes it or not. He has asked the right question of the right person and he is about to get the right answer. He has come to the turning point of his life, and the other Man, you need to notice—the Man in the truly humble clothing with the tired but compassionate eyes standing in front of him—understands the significance of this moment. Jesus knows what is at stake for this rich young ruler.

☙❧

You see, there is a tide in the affairs of Jesus, too. And He is being carried along by the current of God's will on His journey to Jerusalem and the Cross. Jesus knows that this young man will never pass this way again because Jesus Himself will never pass this way again.

This is a divine encounter. This is the moment that will seal this young man's fate—for all eternity. He has come face to face with a Jesus Whose heart goes out to him in love. *"One thing you lack,"* Jesus says. *"Sell what you own and give the money to the poor…then come, follow Me."*

And in that moment, the tide turned.

Kneeling before Jesus—hearing those words and not hearing them—or not believing them—the young man who was close enough to reach out and grasp the hand of Jesus—and through Him, eternal life—found that his own hands and heart would not let go of everything else he had. Jesus extended him an invitation to eternal life, and he refused it because he could not give up the life he had, filled, as it was, with many things. And from that moment on, his life—his prosperous, powerful, prestigious, proper life—became a tragic study in "what might have been."[103]

The man gets up off his knees and turns away from Jesus. He ran to ask his question. He addressed Jesus with eloquent

---

[103] See the 1856 poem, "Maud Muller," by John Greenleaf Whittier.

compliments. Now he walks away—slowly, silently, sadly—with the answer he is unwilling to accept.

"Give it all away," keeps ringing in his ears as he goes back down to his expensive home and his empty life. And Jesus watches him go, sadder than the young man, if that is possible.

Soon Jesus will turn—and resume His journey—a journey up to Jerusalem—up to Calvary—up on a Cross—where Jesus will give everything He owns to the poor of this world—poor sinners who cannot inherit eternal life any other way. Jesus will provide, with His death, the one thing the rich young ruler and every other man and woman in the world lack.

❧

Let's be clear: the one thing the rich young ruler lacked was not poverty. Jesus did not say the man had to be poor. Jesus did not say he could not be rich. Jesus did not tell anyone else to liquidate all his assets and divest himself of all material possessions as a prerequisite for becoming a disciple.

It's the other part: To inherit eternal life, you have to follow Jesus. You have to take up your cross and follow Him.[104]

Jesus had much to teach this man about the kingdom of God in which eternal life is lived. It would take time to teach him, as Jesus was teaching all of His disciples, but time was a luxury Jesus did not have. The man wanted an answer—he wanted eternal life—but he would have to follow Jesus to get it, and he could not bring his stuff along on the journey, because Jesus was on a march to fulfill His mission.

In this case, wealth and power were going to prevent the young man from following Jesus. They did prevent him. And he is not the only one who cannot get around or over or through or past his material possessions to follow Jesus. There is always a great tension between the material and the spiritual—the things of this world

---

[104] Matthew 16:24.

and the things of God.[105] For that reason, submission to the spiritual is more difficult for those with many possessions. Our possessions have a way of possessing us[106] and the process starts early, even in childhood.

The rich, young ruler is not greedy or dishonest or vile. He is simply, in the end, materialistic—too attached to the comfort, status and sense of security his possessions provide. Giving what you have to the poor is a conventionally good and appropriate thing to do with excess resources. So that's how Jesus advises him to eliminate the barrier to eternal life his possessions represent.

And Jesus tells the man he will create a treasure for himself in heaven, just by giving his wealth to the poor—even before he comes to follow Jesus. Of course, it would be a shame to lay up that heavenly treasure by good works and then never see it or enjoy it because you did not follow Jesus and inherit eternal life.

The rich young ruler chooses in the end to hold on to his things, and in so doing, he gives up the one thing that matters most of all. Jesus may not require you to liquidate your assets to follow Him, but He will require you to take a radically different attitude toward what you possess.

You cannot possess the things of the world the way the world has taught you—if you are to be a follower of Jesus. You cannot place them on par with the things of God.[107] You cannot immerse yourself in them to the degree that they prevent you from following Jesus when and where He leads. If what you have gets in the way of your relationship with Jesus, you must get it out of the way[108]—even if it means getting rid of it altogether.

❧❧

---

[105] Romans 8:5-7.
[106] Luke 12:15-21.
[107] Matthew 6:24.
[108] Hebrews 12:1.

But money or material possessions may not be the only things that get in the way. For Peter, it was an unwarranted self-assurance: "I don't need You to wash my feet, Jesus."[109] "I'll never deny You, Jesus."[110]

And Jesus told Peter in the same way He told the rich young ruler: "Get rid of that!"[111]

For Paul, it was a fanatical determination to enforce the Jewish Law, even if it meant chasing down Christians in foreign countries.

Jesus told Paul: "Give it up!"[112]

The point is to eliminate impediments in your journey with Jesus. More than your portfolio, it's about your mindset. The greatest tragedy is that the rich, young ruler thought he couldn't give up his stuff to follow Jesus—to inherit eternal life. But the truth is that what he thought was impossible, God could make possible. God could and would enable him to do it—if the man would let Him.

The truth is, whatever you've got that stands in the way of your following Jesus and inheriting eternal life—whatever barrier between you and God you think is impossible to remove—God can and will remove it, if you let Him. Don't go away grieving. Come and follow Jesus—and inherit eternal life. If there's one thing you lack, God will provide it.

☙❧

---

[109] John 13:6-8.
[110] Mark 14:29, 31.
[111] Mark 14:30.
[112] Acts 9:1-6.

19.

Divine Economics

Mark 12:38-44 NRSV

38 As [Jesus] taught, he said, "Beware of the scribes, who like to walk around in long robes, and to be greeted with respect in the marketplaces, 39 and to have the best seats in the synagogues and places of honor at banquets! 40 They devour widows' houses and for the sake of appearance say long prayers. They will receive the greater condemnation."

41 He sat down opposite the treasury, and watched the crowd putting money into the treasury. Many rich people put in large sums. 42 A poor widow came and put in two small copper coins, which are worth a penny. 43 Then he called his disciples and said to them, "Truly I tell you, this poor widow has put in more than all those who are contributing to the treasury. 44 For all of them have contributed out of their abundance; but she out of her poverty has put in everything she had, all she had to live on."

ळ∞ऽ

They say, "A picture is worth a thousand words," but the Gospel reading today was considerably less than a thousand words, and so you may not have gotten the picture. You saw Jesus, of course, and you heard what He was saying, but the "background" was probably a bit blurry.

Let's bring it into focus.

121

Jesus is in the Temple in Jerusalem—an awe-inspiring architectural complex. It is known throughout the Roman world for its size and beauty. It is known to the Jews, scattered throughout this world, as the holiest place on earth. And Jesus is there.

It is just days before Passover, the great Jewish festival, and hundreds of thousands of Jews have come as pilgrims from around the world to worship in the Temple and celebrate their sacred rites in Jerusalem, their Holy City. They bring with them their religious fervor, their ethnic pride, their political aspirations—and enormous wealth to place at the service of their God.

They have filled Jerusalem. They have crowded into the Temple complex, and many of them are crowded around Jesus. It is noisy. It is cramped. The atmosphere is charged with the sense of excitement—and danger.

People are crowding around Jesus because Jesus is back in the Temple just days after turning the place upside down. He overturned the tables where the pilgrims were supposed to exchange their foreign money for Temple coins. He drove out all the animals that had been brought in for them to buy for sacrifices. He messed up the whole elaborate—and highly profitable—operation, and then added insult to injury by calling the Temple staff running things a "bunch of thieves."

Jesus has crossed some powerful people, and everybody knows they're out to get Him. And yet there He is, walking around the Temple—right under their noses. There He is, in their faces—figuratively—talking about them—and not in flattering terms.

"Beware of the scribes who like to walk around in long robes," Jesus says, shouting to be heard over the din of the place. And looking around, you can see plenty of these guys there in the Temple area. They're walking around in those distinctive long robes. There are even some of them in the crowd listening to Jesus—and they don't look happy.

Scribes. They want to be recognized, but not in the way Jesus is recognizing them. They like to walk around in their special robes so that people will know to bow to them and show them respect. They like to sit up in the special seats on the dais in the synagogue, facing the congregation. They like to sit at the special VIP table at banquets. They love to bask in the attention of a deferential audience of common folk when they cough up some prodigious prayer.

"Who *are* these guys?!"

They are the certified—verified—rarified—experts in the Torah, the Law of Moses. They are professional theologians. They are the spiritual descendants of the Old Testament prophets (to hear them tell it), the special class of men who know the will of God and proclaim it—explain it—and enforce it—whenever and wherever they deem necessary. They are the scribes.

"And what's this business about *'devouring widow's houses'*?" Well, remember that, in the Jewish world of Jesus' day, women do not have legal standing. To take care of his wife, a husband must appoint a trustworthy administrator of his estate to provide for her as a widow, after his death.

But how do you know who will be trustworthy?

Well, a God-fearing man ought to be trustworthy, you reason. And who's the most likely to be God-fearing? Somebody who prays—especially somebody who prays a lot. Who do you know who prays a lot? Well, those scribes in their long robes are always praying; they go on forever.

So...scribes spend a lot of time being estate administrators.

And since they are assumed to be trustworthy, there is little or no outside scrutiny, which allows them to decide for themselves just how much of the estates to pay themselves for managing the estates.

To misquote a phrase: "The fervent prayer of an *un*-righteous man availeth much—in *this* world."[113]

No doubt they pray long and hard—in public—for the poor widows whose resources they are transferring into their own substantial accounts. *"Beware of the scribes,"* Jesus says. "Beware of those who hide greed, pride and the desire for privilege behind a cloak of false piety. Beware of being taken in by them—beware of *becoming* them. They," promises Jesus, "will receive the greater condemnation—from God."

⁊⛤

The crowds have been following Jesus on His walk around the Temple. But now He stops. Does He see something that catches His attention, or has He gotten where He was going all along? He has arrived at a spot opposite the Temple treasury, located in the Court of the Women.

Collection boxes, called "trumpets" because of their shape, are lined up along the wall, each marked for the specific purpose to which the money inside will be directed.

Jesus sits down and watches. He watches people give their offerings to God. And there is a lot of giving. Some very impressive sums make their way into the "trumpets" while Jesus sits and watches. But then Jesus sees something else—something He wants His disciples to see: "Com'ere guys, look at this. This poor widow has put in more than all those who are contributing to the treasury."

Now, maybe this widow had a scribe as an estate manager. Then again, maybe she was just poor. But Jesus is more impressed with the two cents she dropped in the bucket than the big old travelers' checks the prosperous pilgrims had been piling in.

She *"has put in more,"* Jesus says. But more "what"?

---

[113] With apologies to James 5:16, KJV.

Not money. Her offering wouldn't buy a biscuit. The amount of what she gave is nothing compared to what the "big dogs" were doing. More "what"?

The Greek text has a little wrinkle here that most of the English translations, including ours, don't pick up. The Greek says that Jesus *"beheld **how** the crowd put...money into the treasury."* Jesus is not looking at amount; He is looking at attitude. "How" is always more important to God than "how much." So *how* is the widow's "two-bit" offering "more"—more than all the others?

It is more sacrificial. It is not the sum that God looks for—and honors. It is the level of sacrifice. It is the level of sacrifice that tells the tale—that miraculously changes lives and the world. It is sacrifice that embraces the sacrifice of God—that looks to Him for meaning and purpose—and provision—in this life rather than to the luxuries our abundance may afford.

This poor, unknown woman has put in more *sacrifice*—more faith. Others had much and gave some. She has nothing and gives all. Jesus says, *"She has given her whole life."*

But you don't have the whole picture yet.

৯৽৽

Jesus makes a big deal of pointing out this one episode to His disciples. And then Jesus leaves the Temple—never to return. He takes His disciples out of the Temple and tells them it will one day be destroyed.

His public ministry is over. In the time left to Him, Jesus prepares His disciples for His death. And, all the while, the leaders of the Temple are preparing to make His death happen.

And the last thing Jesus showed His disciples in the Temple was not the splendor of its architecture or the holiness of its altar, but a simple woman putting pennies in the Temple version of a collection plate. What did He want them to see?

Maybe Jesus wanted them to see the figure of Someone else Who would give everything He had—His very life—to God, gladly and completely, even though the offering would seem to the world to be of pathetically little value. Maybe Jesus wanted them to remember that even Someone Who appeared poor and helpless, a prime target for powerful and predatory forces, held nothing back when He came to the point of giving what He had.

Jesus showed His disciples a poor widow who took her offering to the Temple just as He would soon take His offering to the Cross—and from there to a Temple *"not made with hands, eternal in the heavens."*[114]

There was precious little the Jerusalem Temple could do with the widow's "mite," her sacrificial offering. But with the equally humble sacrifice Jesus was about to offer, God would change the world and every person, rich or poor, who would come to see what Jesus showed His disciples, first at the treasury in Jerusalem's Temple, and then outside Jerusalem's walls on a hill called Calvary.

Look at her. Do you see what she has done? Do you understand what it means?

The scribes—the professional religious people—were experts in the Law of God, but they did not know the God Who gave the Law, or that God would give Himself as a sacrifice to redeem those who stood condemned by the Law—including them.

Somehow, a poor widow who had not been trained in the Law understood, and she responded in the only proper way: she responded to God's sacrifice for her by sacrificing herself—giving all that she had—to God.

Poor widow?

She was the richest person in the world!

৯৽৽৻

---

[114] 2 Corinthians 5:1, KJV.

From the Book of Hebrews

Hebrews 4:14-16 ESV

[14] *Since then we have a great high priest who has passed through the heavens, Jesus, the Son of God, let us hold fast our confession.* [15] *For we do not have a high priest who is unable to sympathize with our weaknesses, but one who in every respect has been tempted as we are, yet without sin.* [16] *Let us then with confidence draw near to the throne of grace, that we may receive mercy and find grace to help in time of need.*

కా~సి

John 11:47-53 ESV

[47] *So the chief priests and the Pharisees gathered the council and said, "What are we to do? For this man performs many signs.* [48] *If we let him go on like this, everyone will believe in him, and the Romans will come and take away both our place and our nation."* [49] *But one of them, Caiaphas, who was high priest that year, said to them, "You know nothing at all.* [50] *Nor do you understand that it is better for you that one man should die for the people, not that the whole nation should perish."* [51] *He did not say this of his own accord, but being high priest that year he prophesied that Jesus would die for the nation,* [52] *and not for the nation only, but also to gather into one the children of God who are scattered abroad.* [53] *So from that day on they made plans to put [Jesus] to death.*

కా~సి

20.

Sympathetic Intercession

Hebrews 4:14-16; John 11:47-53 ESV

They should have held a parade for Him, after He raised Lazarus from the dead. Instead, they held an emergency meeting and decided to send a posse after Him and make Him as dead as Lazarus had been. "They" were the religious leaders, led by that year's high priest, a fellow named Caiaphas. The "He" the high priest proposed to eliminate was Jesus, just a guy from Galilee Who had this habit of saying things and doing things that inspired the masses and infuriated the elites like Caiaphas.

And it wasn't long before the high priest's posse caught up with Jesus one dark night while He prayed in a garden. And within a day they had "done Him in"—railroaded Him onto a Roman cross where He died a horrible—and sacrificial—death. Jesus became what He had been predicted to be by John the Baptist: *"the Lamb of God Who takes away the sin of the world."* [115] Jesus even became what the high priest inadvertently prophesied He would be: the *"one Man"* Who *"should die for the people...that the whole nation should not perish."*

---

[115] John 1:29, ESV.

And die He did, as Paul wrote in his letter to the Romans: *"...while we were still weak, at the right time Christ died for the ungodly. ...while we were still sinners, Christ died for us."*[116]

But Jesus the Christ did more. He did more than lay down His life as a sacrifice for the sins of the world—the divine Lamb offered by God as the divine Sacrifice to satisfy the requirements of divine righteousness. But to explain the "more" that Jesus did, and is doing even now, I have to tell you more about the ancient system of animal sacrifice—something as alien to us today as—well—aliens.

Since we've never seen the sacrificial system at work, we can be excused for not knowing that the death of the sacrificial victim is only the first part of the process—essential, but not sufficient, in and of itself. The point of killing the animal—a pure, unblemished, innocent animal—was to obtain its blood, the source and substance of its life. This blood—this primal symbol of life—was to be presented to God, on behalf of sinful people, by a priest—an intercessor chosen by God to "go between" God and the people.

Because the priest was also sinful, he had to intercede for his own sins before he could intercede for others. And because no earthly sacrifice was sufficient to cover the continuing sinfulness of the people, the priest would have to offer sacrifices over and over again.

The greatest sacrifice that could be offered was offered once a year, by the high priest, who alone took the blood of a sacrificed animal through a veil—a huge, heavy curtain separating people from the holiest place there was—the place where God caused His divine glory to reside.[117] The high priest came into the presence of the glory of God and presented to God the blood of life that had been taken from an animal—he presented it by sprinkling it on God's holy altar. And as soon as the high priest had done this, he

---

[116] Romans 5:6, 8, ESV.
[117] Deuteronomy 16:2; 1 Kings 8:10-11.

retreated from the Holy of Holies, not to return until the same day on the following year.

It was not safe for anyone else to pass through the veil into the Holy of Holies at any time. It was not safe for the high priest to enter the Holy of Holies any other day of the year. It was not safe for the high priest to remain in the presence of the glory of God after he had offered the sacrifice. This was a God Who could "take you out" in less time than it takes a bolt of lightning to flash. But to complete the sacrifice and to have it be sufficient for the atonement of the people—even for a year—the high priest had to present the sacrificial blood to God.

But if you did the job right—according to the rules—you would probably be all right. Even old Caiaphas apparently made it in and out of the Holy of Holies unharmed.

The sacrificial system kept working right up to the destruction of the Temple by a Roman army in 70 A.D. However, according to the author of the Book of Hebrews, offering sacrifices in the Temple had been unnecessary for about 40 years before that, ever since Jesus bid His followers farewell and ascended into heaven some 40 days after His Resurrection.[118]

According to Hebrews, Jesus didn't go to heaven just to "hang out" forever. He went to finish what He started on the Cross. Or perhaps, I should say "continue," because Jesus is even now interceding for us—covering our sins with His blood—doing the work of the great and final High Priest for us every moment of every day until we join Him in heaven and there is no longer any need for anybody to intercede for us ever again because when we are in heaven with Jesus we will never sin again.

Now, don't get me wrong. The Crucifixion of Jesus was the "full, perfect and sufficient sacrifice, oblation and satisfaction for the sins of the whole world"[119] given by God for our redemption. Nobody but Jesus could have made that sacrifice and have it be

---

[118] Acts 1:9.

[119] From *The Episcopal Book of Common Prayer*, 1928.

valid, because nobody but Jesus ever lived the sinless life that was necessary to be a Lamb of God Who *could* take away the sins of the world.[120] And nobody can or needs to add anything to what Jesus did in dying on the Cross to satisfy the requirements of righteousness.

But the One Who *was* the sacrifice—Who *made* the sacrifice—became, by the will and commission of God, the One Who, as a newly appointed High Priest, would *offer* the sacrifice to God on our behalf. Because of the Blood He shed (and now offers as the all-sufficient and acceptable sacrifice to God the Father), Jesus the Son of God atones for every sin that has been committed or will be committed—by every person who holds fast to his or her confession—the confession that Jesus Christ is Savior and Lord—and great High Priest interceding for us.

And look at the difference between Jesus, our great High Priest, and any other priest. All the other priests offered sacrifices in a tabernacle or a temple, in an earthly place God chose to make holy. Jesus offers His sacrifice at the very throne of God in heaven—in the very presence of God. Other priests went through a curtain made to look like heaven.[121] Jesus went through heaven itself. He intercedes for us with a God He does not have to fear. He is in all ways, and for all time and beyond, pleasing to His Father.

Other priests had only the blood of animals to offer on their altars. Jesus has His own shed Blood with which to wash away our sins. Human priests have to cover their own sins. Jesus has no sin of His own to cover. All He does at the throne of God in heaven He does for us.

And He does it sympathetically.

---

[120] John 1:29.
[121] Described by Josephus in his *Jewish War*, 5.5.4., p. 212-14. See also David Ulansey, "The Heavenly Veil Torn: Mark's Cosmic Inclusio," *Journal of Biblical Literature*, Vol. 110, No. 1 (Spring, 1991), pp. 123-125.

"Sympathy," in Bible times, did not mean exactly what it does today. More than an attitude or feeling of concern, it meant "to suffer with"—"to suffer alongside"—"to suffer the same thing." It is to feel what someone else feels because you're in the same situation together. Our great High Priest—Who intercedes directly with God in heaven—knows, understands and appreciates what we're going through and dealing with because He has gone through it and dealt with it, too.

Was He hungry or thirsty? Probably more often than any of us have ever been.

Was He tired? Most of the time, He got no time off, and we know He fell asleep at least once in the middle of a storm at sea.

Was He ever afraid? There was plenty to be afraid of in His world and He prayed for deliverance in the Garden like a Man Who knew He was in danger.

Was He ever tempted? More than you and me because when we yield to temptation, it goes away for a while. Jesus never yielded, and so the pressure of resisted temptations just grew and grew beyond anything we have ever known.

Jesus is able *"to sympathize with our weaknesses"*—moral and spiritual, as well as physical—and so He intercedes for us with sympathy—with understanding, compassion and concern, because He's been where we are. The only difference between His experience of life on this earth and ours is that He did not sin.

Because He did not sin in this life, Jesus *can* atone for our sins. Because He endured in full measure what we experience in this life, He *wants* to intercede for us.

And He does. But we must not let our commitment to Him slip. *"Let us hold fast our confession,"* the inspired author of Hebrews urges.

And he urges us to do one other thing in response to our Lord's sympathetic intercession: "Come and get it!"

"Let us draw near with confidence to the throne of grace"—which without the effective intercession of Christ would be the throne of

judgment—*"Let us draw near with confidence...that we may receive mercy and find grace to help in time of need."*

Your place is up front where Jesus is interceding for you—right there in front of God the Father—*His* Father, and, as a result of His intercession—*your* Father.

Don't be shy. Don't be afraid. Don't be ashamed of what you have done in your life. Your sympathetic Intercessor—your great High Priest—knows all about that and has taken care of it with God so that you can come into God's presence with confidence that you are loved and accepted, and your sins are atoned for.

Want mercy?

You got it!

Need grace?

There's more grace here, of every kind, than you can imagine, and more than enough to take care of all the problems you have, or could have in a million lifetimes. Grace pours out of this heavenly throne because the God Who occupies it is the Source of all grace and gives grace without limit for the sake of the One interceding at the throne for you.

Jesus is interceding for you right now. Hold fast your faith in Him. Draw near with confidence to Him. Receive God's mercy through Him and find the grace you need.

&-&

Hebrews 5:1-10 NRSV

[1] *Every high priest chosen from among mortals is put in charge of things pertaining to God on their behalf, to offer gifts and sacrifices for sins.* [2] *He is able to deal gently with the ignorant and wayward, since he himself is subject to weakness;* [3] *and because of this he must offer sacrifice for his own sins as well as for those of the people.* [4] *And one does not presume to take this honor, but takes it only when called by God, just as Aaron was.*

[5] *So also Christ did not glorify himself in becoming a high priest, but was appointed by the one who said to him,*

> *"You are my Son, today I have begotten you";*

[6] *as he says also in another place,*

> *"You are a priest forever, according to the order of Melchizedek."*

[7] *In the days of his flesh, Jesus offered up prayers and supplications, with loud cries and tears, to the one who was able to save him from death, and he was heard because of his reverent submission.* [8] *Although he was a Son, he learned obedience through what he suffered;* [9] *and having been made perfect, he became the source of eternal salvation for all who obey him,* [10] *having been designated by God a high priest according to the order of Melchizedek.*

৵৹৶

21.

Learning Obedience

Hebrews 5:1-10 NRSV

You're going to have to stay with me today. We've got heavy stuff to talk about. No jokes—no laughter—just Hebrews, Chapter 5. And for our purposes, just two verses—8 and 9: *"Though being a Son, Jesus learned, from the things he suffered, obedience. And being perfected, he became, to all who are obeying him, the source of eternal salvation."*

Now it's hard to imagine Jesus needing to learn anything. Sure, Luke says, *"Jesus increased in wisdom"* (among other things) as He was growing up.[122] But by the time He was grown and about His ministry, Jesus was the One doing the teaching.[123] What did He have to learn?

Certainly not obedience. Nobody was more committed to obedience than Jesus. It wasn't like He needed help getting from disobedience to obedience, or from a little obedience to more obedience. Still, it says Jesus learned obedience through what He suffered.

Let's consider this business of obedience. It's easy to be obedient when you are directed to do something you want to do anyway. It's still relatively easy to obey when you are told to do

---

[122] Luke 2:52, NRSV.
[123] Mark 1:22.

something you're not opposed to doing, even if you don't have a desire to do it already.

But obedience takes on a different meaning when you're given an assignment you would never do unless you were told to. And when you're told to do the last thing in the world you would want to do, your obedience teaches you something you could not learn any other way. You learn what obedience *means*. In His suffering, Jesus learned what His commitment to obedience meant, in a way no theoretical understanding could convey.

And because of His obedience, something happened that would never have happened if He had not been completely obedient. Jesus became the Source or Cause of eternal salvation, not based on His obedience, but on His suffering, suffering that He would not have endured if He had wavered in His obedience to God under the fear or the pain of what He was to suffer.

And the culmination of that suffering was His death on the Cross.[124] The Crucifixion completed a Life that experienced all the temptations known to man—all the temptation, and yet none of the sin.[125] Jesus was living a perfect life every day of His life, but it wasn't until His life was over—which it wasn't until Calvary—it wasn't until then that He was *perfected* as the Source of our salvation.

In the completion of the suffering He obediently accepted, Jesus achieved our salvation…

⁂

…*if*, that is to say, *we* are not rejecting it, by being *dis*obedient to *Him*. The Book of Hebrews is written to people who are learning that obedience to Jesus requires *them* to suffer, too.[126] They are learning what Christian obedience means in terms of suffering. And they don't like it.

---

[124] John 19:28-30.
[125] Hebrews 4:15.
[126] Hebrews 10:32-36.

But they must also learn that there is no salvation without that suffering because there is no salvation without the obedience of Jesus to the Father and our obedience (to the degree that faith makes our obedience possible) to Jesus. Jesus learned that, even being the Son of God, His commitment to obedience to God His Father still required great suffering from Him.

Jesus is now the perfected Son of God Who has made us perfectly acceptable *to* God—*through* His suffering. Jesus has made us sons and daughters of God—but only if we are exercising the faith that enables us to obey Him—and follow Him—and trust in Him—even in the midst of suffering.[127]

But an interesting thing happens when you continue to obey Jesus in spite of the suffering this obedience entails. You learn the *meaning* of *your* obedience. Your commitment to obedience moves from theoretical to experiential. You understand your suffering within the framework of your salvation. You see *your* suffering in the light of *His* suffering.[128]

We learn obedience from Him as we experience suffering—and our eternal salvation—in Him.

৯৽৺

---

[127] Romans 5:1-5.
[128] 2 Corinthians 1:5; Philippians 3:7-11.

Hebrews 9:11-14 NRSV

¹¹ But when Christ came as a high priest of the good things that have come, then through the greater and perfect tent (not made with hands, that is, not of this creation), ¹² he entered once for all into the Holy Place, not with the blood of goats and calves, but with his own blood, thus obtaining eternal redemption. ¹³ For if the blood of goats and bulls, with the sprinkling of the ashes of a heifer, sanctifies those who have been defiled so that their flesh is purified, ¹⁴ how much more will the blood of Christ, who through the eternal Spirit offered himself without blemish to God, purify our conscience from dead works to worship the living God!

అ•అ

22.

Nothing But the Blood of Jesus

Hebrews 9:11-14 NRSV

Late in the month of August, in the year 70 A.D., Roman legions set fire to the great Temple in Jerusalem.[129] It was one of the final acts in their campaign to crush a four-year-old Jewish uprising against them.

The destruction of the Temple also ended the practice of animal sacrifice that had been central to the Jewish religion. These blood sacrifices, offered to atone for the sins of the Jewish people, were first conducted on that Temple Mount over a thousand years earlier when Solomon dedicated the new Temple he had built by sacrificing 22,000 oxen and 120,000 sheep to God.[130] And every day for centuries before that at village shrines—and earlier still, in their sacred tent in the desert—God's people had sacrificed animals for their sins.[131]

But on that August day in 70 A.D., all that ended. From that day to this, there has been no system of animal sacrifice for the atonement of sin.

---

[129] Josephus, *The Wars of the Jews or History of the Destruction of Jerusalem*, written about 110 AD.
[130] 2 Chronicles 7:5.
[131] Leviticus 9; 1 Samuel 1.

And just as well, according to the Book of Hebrews, because these animal sacrifices were, at best, "make do"—temporary and partial fixes for a problem that wasn't going to go away. God told them to sacrifice the animals—so there was some good purpose in it.

They gave up their animals to pay for their sins. And this was a gracious option from God, because the alternative was to give up their own lives.[132] Those who sin against God deserve to die.[133] Sounds harsh—but that's the way it is. So they took the generous option and sacrificed their animals, and gave thanks that that was all they had to give up.

But shedding the blood of their animals did not fix the root problem that made the sacrifices necessary. These sacrifices covered the flesh—protected their physical selves—dealt with what they "did." But they didn't get at "why" people did sinful things in the first place. The sacrifices didn't change the people inside.

We've never been a part of an animal sacrifice system; we've never depended on the blood of goats and bulls to improve our relationship with God. For us, the whole idea is pretty gross—and we don't have to be card-carrying PETA people to feel that way.

But we are no different from those people in our basic, primal sinfulness. We have the same hearts and minds and inclinations they had.[134] And so, we have the same problem with God—and the same need. The reason we don't cut up animals as our way of worship is not because the Temple is gone. We are the beneficiaries of a better system of sacrifice.

Where the blood of innocent animals was once poured out each day in a holy tent in the desert or at the Temple in Jerusalem, the blood of Jesus, the innocent Son of God, has been poured out

---

[132] Exodus 34:18-20.
[133] Romans 3:23.
[134] Genesis 6:5.

once for all upon the ultimate altar in heaven, of which all the altars on earth have been but faint and feeble imitations.

And where the blood of animals could, at best, only keep God "off your back" for a day, the blood of Jesus, shed for you and offered up for you, brings you into the eternal embrace of God and brings God into your heart, now and forever.

"The blood of Christ," it says in Hebrews, *"[will] purify our conscience..."* His sacrifice brings atonement of body and soul. His blood bought our full and eternal redemption.

How does that song go?

> "What can wash away my sin?
> What can make me whole again?"[135]

Now you know the answer: "Nothing but the blood of Jesus."

> "Nothing can for sin atone—
> nothing good that I have done.
> Nothing...but the blood of Jesus."

❧

---

[135] From the hymn "What Can Wash Away My Sin," Robert Lowry, 1876.

143

Hebrews 10:11-14, 19-25 NRSV

¹¹ And every priest stands day after day at his service, offering again and again the same sacrifices that can never take away sins. ¹² But when Christ had offered for all time a single sacrifice for sins, "he sat down at the right hand of God," ¹³ and since then has been waiting "until his enemies would be made a footstool for his feet." ¹⁴ For by a single offering he has perfected for all time those who are sanctified. ¹⁵ And the Holy Spirit also testifies to us, for after saying,

> *¹⁶ "This is the covenant that I will make with them after those days, says the Lord:*
>
> > *I will put my laws in their hearts,*
> > *and I will write them on their minds,"*
>
> *¹⁷ he also adds,*
>
> > *"I will remember their sins*
> > *and their lawless deeds no more."*

¹⁸ Where there is forgiveness of these, there is no longer any offering for sin.

¹⁹ Therefore, my friends, since we have confidence to enter the sanctuary by the blood of Jesus, ²⁰ by the new and living way that he opened for us through the curtain (that is, through his flesh), ²¹ and since we have a great priest over the house of God, ²² let us approach with a true heart in full assurance of faith, with our hearts sprinkled clean from an evil conscience and our bodies washed with pure water. ²³ Let us hold fast to the confession of our hope without wavering, for he who has promised is faithful. ²⁴ And let us consider how to provoke one another to love and good deeds, ²⁵ not neglecting to meet together, as is the habit of some, but encouraging one another, and all the more as you see the Day approaching.

ॐ

23.

The Image of a Different World

Hebrews 10:11-14; 19-25 NRSV

When I was a younger man, I sat in front of a TV set and watched the world as I had always known it disappear, and a new world take its place. What I saw stunned me because I had always thought what I saw was completely impossible. And yet, there it was, happening right before my eyes.

I saw people climbing up on concrete slabs. I saw them pounding the concrete with hammers. I saw bulldozers shoving the slabs over. I saw the Berlin Wall come down.

I remember thinking at the time that seeing those images was more stunning to me than watching men walk on the moon 20 years before. I always believed men would walk on the moon. When they did, I was excited, but I was not stunned. I was not even surprised.

But I never thought "the wall" would come down. When it did, I knew I was living in a different world.

❧❦

The old world disappeared and a new one took its place with the things the book of Hebrews described. And that change was far more significant than what happened in 1989.

What happened almost 2,000 years ago was also something nobody thought could happen. Did it look like the most amazing thing in the world when it happened? No, it just looked like a cruel but commonplace act: the execution of a troublesome man.

But amazing it was!

If you pay attention to what's being said in this tenth chapter of Hebrews, and recognize its significance, you may—and should—be stunned. In verse 12, it says, *"…Christ…offered—for all time—a single sacrifice for sins."* And then, in verse 14, it says, *"…by a single offering, He has perfected—for all time—those who are sanctified."*

Men going to the moon and walking around was a remarkable achievement, but that was nothing compared to the Creator of the moon and everything else in the universe coming to earth as a man and walking among us.

Tearing down a wall that held an entire nation captive for a generation in the iron grip of communism was a stunning development. But tearing down the barrier that held all humanity in the death grip of sin—that separated every person from God since the beginning of time—was a far greater development. It was the greatest event in the history of the world.

By a single offering of a single sacrifice for sins—by one offering, good for all time—Christ has "perfected" those who are "sanctified"—for all time. Those who are "sanctified" (who have been set apart from the rest of humanity to be related to God and to interact with God in the special way God desires and determines) have been "perfected" (made exactly what God wants them to be so that they are completely capable of relating to God and interacting with God as He desires).

And these special people will always be exactly what God wants them to be—and will always be able to relate to God and interact with God exactly as God wants them to—because Christ has offered that one, for-all-time, special sacrifice for sins—perfecting them.

And why are these special people sanctified—set apart—while other people are not? How is it that they are "perfected" by this one, once-for-all sacrifice of Himself by Jesus, and everybody else is not?

Simple, really. They—the "sanctified"—are the people who look at what has happened—who look at the sacrifice Jesus has offered—and are willing to believe that it means the old world they knew is gone and a new world has taken its place.

Sometimes, something that can't possibly happen does. Sometimes, the world you've always known disappears right before your eyes, and a new world you never imagined takes its place.

When God makes the impossible happen, believe and act accordingly. When you see Jesus knock down the wall of sin and death with His sacrifice, come out of that old world of bondage and into the new one where you will have been perfected and sanctified. Be set apart—be transformed—be God's—for all time—now and forever.

৵৽

Hebrews 11:1-2, 13-16, 39-40 ESV

¹ Now faith is the assurance of things hoped for, the conviction of things not seen. ² For by it the people of old received their commendation.

¹³ These all died in faith, not having received the things promised, but having seen them and greeted them from afar, and having acknowledged that they were strangers and exiles on the earth. ¹⁴ For people who speak thus make it clear that they are seeking a homeland. ¹⁵ If they had been thinking of that land from which they had gone out, they would have had opportunity to return. ¹⁶ But as it is, they desire a better country, that is, a heavenly one. Therefore God is not ashamed to be called their God, for he has prepared for them a city.

³⁹ And all these, though commended through their faith, did not receive what was promised, ⁴⁰ since God had provided something better for us, that apart from us they should not be made perfect.

෧෮ඁ෮

John 5:24-29 ESV

[Jesus said:]
²⁴ "Truly, truly, I say to you, whoever hears my word and believes him who sent me has eternal life. He does not come into judgment, but has passed from death to life.

²⁵ "Truly, truly, I say to you, an hour is coming, and is now here, when the dead will hear the voice of the Son of God, and those who hear will live. ²⁶ For as the Father has life in himself, so he has granted the Son also to have life in himself. ²⁷ And he has given him authority to execute judgment, because he is the Son of Man. ²⁸ Do not marvel at this, for an hour is coming when all who are in the tombs will hear his voice ²⁹ and come out, those who have done good to the resurrection of life, and those who have done evil to the resurrection of judgment."

෧෮ඁ෮

24.

Faith and Faithfulness

Hebrews 11:1-2, 13-16, 39-40; John 5:24-29 ESV

Well, the plan was to preach you a wonderful sermon on faith and faithfulness from this wonderful passage in Hebrews that starts off by defining faith and finishes up with a lengthy list of very faithful people. The first step in the preparation process was to look up key words in the original language to get a better sense of how they were used in biblical times. Sometimes, they didn't mean exactly what we mean by the English words we use to translate them.

So I looked up what the writer of Hebrews said "faith" was. The translation you heard said, *"...faith is the assurance of things hoped for, the conviction of things not seen."* And that's very inspiring. But that's not really what the words the writer of Hebrews used actually meant—not all of them, anyway.

He did say, *"...faith is..."* And he did say faith has something to do with *"things hoped for"* and *"things not seen."* The problem in translation is with the part about "assurance" and "conviction." As wonderful as those words are—and as much as I would encourage you to have assurance and conviction when it comes to what you believe about Jesus—that's not really what the Book of Hebrews says "faith" is.

And our translation is not the only one that got it wrong. My old favorite, the Revised Standard Version, gives the same words: "assurance" and "conviction"—as does the very literal New American Standard Bible. The New International Version of the 1970s uses different words to say the same thing, as do several other modern translations.

The old King James Version, on the other hand, got it right. It reads *"...faith is the **substance** of things hoped for—the **evidence** of things not seen."*

❧

What's the difference? And what's the big deal?

"Assurance" and "conviction"—and words like them—are subjective terms; they describe your feelings or attitudes. Words like these tell you what your faith *ought* to be like. They make it sound like Hebrews is defining "faith" as the quality of your personal experience, or the level of your religious commitment. And that's not the point at all.

The writer of Hebrews is dealing in cold, hard, objective facts. What he is saying is that faith is not your feeling of assurance, but the divine substance of existence—the ultimate reality of the universe—the eternal, unalterable truth that God has revealed in Jesus Christ—the substance, reality and truth that will remain when everything else in this world and all Creation is long gone.

"Faith" in the Book of Hebrews is not how assured or confident you feel, but the incredible reality of God that makes your assurance possible and appropriate, and without which, any assurance on your part would be ridiculous. Everything you've been taught by sacred scripture about Jesus and what He accomplished by His sacrificial death and supernatural Resurrection is the substance of the Christian faith and is the only truth worthy of your trust and the commitment of your life.

Nothing on your part or anyone else's can make the *substance* of this faith you put your trust in more substantial or more trustworthy. Nothing you or anyone else in all the world say or do can diminish it from its status as the only ultimate reality among all the temporary impressions of reality that promise what they cannot produce.

Faith is the reality of the things you've been taught to hope for—to look forward to. It is not whatever assurance you feel about whatever you believe in.

⤜⤛

Nor, according to Hebrews, is faith any conviction you might have about things you have not seen. The "things" of a supernatural God—His thoughts and His ways—are also supernatural, and so you would expect that, as the Prophet Isaiah wrote,

> *"My thoughts are not your thoughts,*
> *Nor are your ways my ways,"*
> *declares the* LORD.
> *"For as the heavens are higher than the earth,*
> *So are my ways higher than your ways*
> *And my thoughts than your thoughts."*[136]

In other words, you would expect that the things of God would be things you would not normally "see." But rather than being your subjective, personal conviction about things you have not seen, "faith" turns out to be objective *evidence* of those things. God gives demonstrations of the supernatural substance of the reality of His salvation in ways and places that you *can* see. God provides proof of the gospel for those who will see it. The great mystery of the ages, says Paul in Ephesians, has now been revealed for all to see.[137] If you have conviction about what you believe, it is because God revealed to you the supernatural reality about which you are convinced.

---

[136] Isaiah 55:8-9, RSV.
[137] Ephesians 1:7-10.

So "faith," for Hebrews, is the true, objective, and ultimate reality that God has established in Jesus Christ. And "faith" is the many simple and dramatic demonstrations of God's will and work throughout history, culminating in His redemption of sinful humanity through Jesus Christ.

Jesus Christ is the basic essence of this faith and the greatest evidence of this faith.

Those are the objective facts.

❧

But is there no subjective side to this faith? Is there no place for things like assurance and conviction?

Hebrews, Chapter 11, proceeds from this definition of faith to a litany of personal profiles, each an example of faith—*and* faithfulness. Each man or woman mentioned put his or her faith in the faithfulness of God even before the ultimate Substance and greatest Demonstration of faith was revealed.

Far more than the New Testament generation—and more still than our generation—those who lived before Christ had to hope for a reality that would not be revealed in their lifetimes. Abel and Enoch, Abraham and all the others saw the evidence of God's faithfulness in their days without seeing the ultimate Proof to which all the divine demonstrations were pointing.

And still they believed.

And they lived toward God with all the assurance and conviction they could muster. They embraced God's faith in their times and trusted that His promises to them would be kept, then or beyond. They chose faith and were as faithful as they were able to be. And for God, it was enough.

In the words of Hebrews, they *"received their commendation."* And, for that reason, their faith in this faith has paid off, even centuries after their deaths. The objective truth of the Christian faith and the subjective response of individuals to this reality in every age—past, present and future—are the two essential elements of God's divine plan.

"They all died in faith," which is a good thing, because even though they died *"not having received the things promised,"* which seems like a bad thing, the chapter concludes by saying that *"God had provided something better for us, that apart from us they should not be made perfect,"* which sounds like a confusing thing, until you untangle the translation and realize that what he is saying is that "together with us, they *shall* be made perfect." Everyone who put his or her faith in God *before* Jesus will be made just as perfect as *you* will be as someone who has put your faith in God because you have lived *after* Jesus, and know from personal experience Who to believe in.

God has given you a faith to believe in—a reality that is the true and all-sufficient fulfillment of His historic promise of salvation. God has been faithful to the people of every age.

And He calls you to embrace this faith and live in faithfulness to Him as He has always been—and will always be—faithful to you.

Rest assured: It's *"the substance of things hoped for"*—the convincing *"evidence of things* (otherwise) *unseen."*

⧫⧫⧫

Hebrews 12:5-11 ESV

The Book of Hebrews was written at a time when Christians were facing growing hostility from the world. The writer points to a father's responsibility to mold and shape the character and faith of his children as an example of what God is doing in the lives of Christians as we endure the opposition of our culture.

❧

⁵ And have you forgotten the exhortation that addresses you as sons?
"My son, do not regard lightly the discipline of the Lord,
nor be weary when reproved by him.
⁶ For the Lord disciplines the one he loves,
and chastises every son whom he receives."
⁷ It is for discipline that you have to endure. God is treating you as sons. For what son is there whom his father does not discipline? ⁸ If you are left without discipline, in which all have participated, then you are illegitimate children and not sons. ⁹ Besides this, we have had earthly fathers who disciplined us and we respected them. Shall we not much more be subject to the Father of spirits and live? ¹⁰ For they disciplined us for a short time as it seemed best to them, but he disciplines us for our good, that we may share his holiness. ¹¹ For the moment all discipline seems painful rather than pleasant, but later it yields the peaceful fruit of righteousness to those who have been trained by it.

❧

Build Your House

Matthew 7:24-27 ESV

Jesus concludes the Sermon on the Mount with a comparison of the results of building on solid as opposed to shifting foundations. The lesson applies to building physical houses—and to building faith and families as well.

ᐒ᎒

[Jesus said:]

24 *"Everyone then who hears these words of mine and does them will be like a wise man who built his house on the rock.* 25 *And the rain fell, and the floods came, and the winds blew and beat on that house, but it did not fall, because it had been founded on the rock.* 26 *And everyone who hears these words of mine and does not do them will be like a foolish man who built his house on the sand.* 27 *And the rain fell, and the floods came, and the winds blew and beat against that house, and it fell, and great was the fall of it."*

ᐒ᎒

25.

Build Your House

Hebrews 12:5-11; Matthew 7:24-27 ESV

The fabric of society is fraying. Our culture is coming apart. And when, in the decades to come, scavengers rummage among the ruins of "what used to be," and wonder why it all came crashing down, they may not realize that the answer was as simple as this: Fathers did not bother to build their "houses." Or if they did—when they did—they built on sand rather than rock.

You can see the advancing images of this terrifying future in the news reports and entertainment offerings of our day: the acceptance and legalization of mood- and mind-altering drug use; the rising frequency and ferocity of violence by organized gangs and random individuals; the acceptance and celebration of immorality disguised as a brave and noble commitment to equality and tolerance; the intensifying hostility to Christianity and growing efforts on many fronts to curtail its activities and influence; the widespread neglect and rejection of marriage as the gateway to sexual activity and the proper environment for children to be conceived and nurtured.

But behind all this is a pattern of fathers not building their "houses"—their families—on solid rock.

It is not my intention or desire to beat up on the fathers who are here today. On Mothers' Day, moms get heaps of praise and gratitude. On Fathers' Day, dads should not get dumped on.

But let me put the challenge you're facing as fathers—Christian fathers—in perspective, and help you equip yourself for your God-given responsibility and privilege. And even more importantly, let me talk to mothers and fathers (and grandparents, aunts and uncles) of boys who will grow into men—*if* they are raised with a discerning appreciation of what they are being raised for—*if* they are led to see the godly purpose of their manhood. Helping them see that purpose is your responsibility.

All across our country, for a generation and more, boys have been allowed to grow up physically without being formed into men—without being disciplined, trained and required—forced, where necessary—to become men at the end of their adolescence. Our society has encouraged the extension of childhood beyond high school, beyond college, beyond the decade of the 20s.

And so, a multitude of male human beings, old enough to be men, but allowed to remain boys, emotionally, psychologically, and morally—have undermined the foundation of our society by omission and commission—by failing to be and act like men—by remaining boys and acting like it. In our permissive society, where technology has reduced the natural consequences of immoral acts, and secularism has removed their stigma, boys in their teens (and 20s and 30s) feel free to enjoy the pleasures of manhood without accepting the responsibilities that men should shoulder. And as any immature child will do, they take what is at hand with no thought for the consequences, to themselves or others.

And they have been abetted in their immaturity and immorality by parents who are too much focused on meeting material needs, and too much afraid to oppose the rising tide of immorality around them. The perpetual male adolescent has been abetted in his moral irresponsibility by foolish girls who value attention and popularity more than their virtue and the better future they have been deceived into throwing away. And worst of all, the abettors are the leaders of institutions who create the environments of immorality that boys and men-who-will-not-grow-up exist in and adapt their perspectives and behaviors to.

And so there is in our country a growing epidemic of children conceived by fathers who have no ability and no desire to fulfill their paternal responsibilities. There is a growing epidemic of child-men who will not marry the women who bear their children, or will not remain faithful to them if they do marry them at some point. There is a growing epidemic of men—including men in the military and on college campuses—assaulting girls and women who will not consent to their sexual advances—or perhaps assaulting them because consent has become so commonplace that it is insufficiently stimulating for those whose only goal in life is to see how much they can get away with.

And, as a result, more and more families are built without fathers—or with the poorest excuses for fathers—by women who are financially handicapped and emotionally wounded, for children who were the product, not of selfless love and lifelong commitment, but of immaturity, irresponsibility and indifference to the innocent and helpless lives that would result from immoral and irresponsible behavior.

And more and more children are growing up in homes without the sacrificial example and positive moral discipline of strong godly fathers. A generation of immature men and women has grown up—or *not* grown up—using each other to satisfy selfish interests and receiving no genuine affirmation in the process. Violence increases and trust decreases across our country. Everyone, victim and victimizer alike, ends up alone. And society unravels like a fabric from which individual threads are systematically removed…

☙❧

…which is why things must change—why fathers must build their "houses"—their families—and build them on the solid rock of Jesus. Our society's future will be determined by the future of our families, and the future of our families will be determined by the moral and spiritual foundations of the men who are and will become our families' fathers. It is as simple and significant as that.

And Jesus said, *"Everyone who hears these words of Mine and puts them into practice is like a wise man who built his house on the rock."*

Fathers—and fathers-to-be: Your families, now and for generations to come, will be made strong and successful by your hearing and practicing what Jesus has said, more than anything else. The happiness of your wives and the wellbeing of your children, and of their children, and of their children's children when you are long in your grave, will be determined, in large measure, by how well you build your own spiritual foundation on Jesus.

That's the first part of a two-part process. There happiness and wellbeing will also depend on how well you establish your marriage and your family on that same foundation in the time God allots to you.

When Jesus used this example of building a house, He was talking about a physical structure. But in the Bible, a man's "house" has often meant his family, those living under his roof and those who will be his descendants forever after him. God told King David, "You will not build Me a house, but I will build you a house—*I will raise up your offspring to succeed you, your own flesh and blood....*"[138] And so God did, till the House of David produced the Savior of the world.

The Psalmist wrote, *"Unless the LORD builds the house, the builders labor in vain,"*[139] which seems to imply that without God's help, a father cannot build his house successfully—cannot put the proper foundation under his marriage or his family. Without God's help

---

[138] 2 Samuel 7:12, NIV.
[139] Psalm 127:1, NIV.

and guidance, a father's best intentions will fail. "All other ground," as the hymn says, "is sinking sand."[140]

C. S. Lewis once wrote, "There are lots of nice things you can do with sand: but do not try building a house on it."[141] And Jesus said it was the foolish man who built his house on the sand, because that house, and every house, is going to be hit by the powerful storms of life. The house on the rock stands, but the house on sand is blown away. And so I repeat: "All other ground is sinking sand."

Build your house on the Rock. Anchor your life—anchor your marriage—anchor your children, sons and daughters alike—on the Rock Who enables you and them to withstand every storm.

"But I'm not really that religious."

Then *get* "religious"—for the sake of your house, your family, your future. Get some solid Rock under you for a change, and the sooner the better.

In other words, let Jesus make God your Father; let Jesus make *you* God's son. And then make your heavenly Father your model for fatherhood. Let Jesus help you grow up into spiritual maturity as a man of God—whatever your age.

❧

So how will you build your house, now that you are a father—or when you become a father? The secret is: divinely inspired discipline.

The reading in Hebrews says, *"Endure hardship as discipline."* For the sake of your children, accept the hardships you encounter with manly maturity. God corrects us when we do wrong—for our benefit. And even when we do right, God uses the difficulties we

---

[140] From the hymn, "The Solid Rock," Edward Mote (lyrics, 1834), William B. Bradbury (tune, 1863).
[141] C. S. Lewis, *Mere Christianity*, (The Complete C. S. Lewis Signature Classics), Zondervan: Grand Rapids, MI, 2007, p.154.

experience in life (through no fault of our own) to form us and strengthen us and make us better men.

Do the same with your sons and daughters. Do not be afraid to correct what is wrong, and do not be too quick to remove all difficulty from their path, for you will not always be there to do so, and the strength and wisdom gained in facing hardships and disappointments in childhood build character and maturity for adulthood later on.

The mission of every boy is to become a godly man so that, if it is God's will, he is ready and able to build his own house—his own family—under the Fatherhood of God. Make sure that your sons know that, and that nothing in their experience of childhood prevents them or delays them from progressing toward manhood and maturity in their proper time.

Teach your sons that the daughters of other fathers are to be respected as the partners they will become for some man in the future. Girls and women are not to be treated as objects of conquest to be collected and discarded as opportunity allows. Teach your son that some father's daughter will grow up to be *his* wife and partner for life—the woman who will bear the children God chooses to give him—and that he must devote himself to becoming the man who is worthy of such a priceless gift. Discipline your son if you would be a wise and godly father.

And if you are a father of daughters, discipline them as well. Show them the respect and selfless love they should expect and demand from every boy and man they encounter as they grow up. Treat their mothers with that same respect and love. Do not let your daughters define themselves, at any age, in attitude, actions or appearance, as less than what God has created them to be. Show them what a man who has built his house on the solid Rock looks like and lives like—and how they may depend on him.

Some of you fathers are doing these things already. I have seen you. You have placed your life and your marriage and your family on the strong and safe foundation. You are building your house on the Rock. Your sons are becoming men who will be worthy of godly women, and your daughters are becoming women who will be worthy of godly men.

But there are too many foolish men—and too many boys who should be men—building too many houses on sand. We need more men—more fathers—to build their houses on the solid Rock.

Pray that God will turn our nation's boys into men and our men into wise and godly fathers, for the sake of their children— and the society that cannot survive otherwise.

❧

26.

The Same Jesus Christ

Hebrews 13:8 NRSV

⁸ Jesus Christ is the same yesterday and today and forever.

෴

The hand of an unknown writer dips a pen into ink and scratches a few simple words on the page before him. He has been writing for hours—days—perhaps weeks. He is near the end of his monumental effort—an inspired argument carefully crafted for a particular group of people on the verge of destroying themselves spiritually in a shortsighted attempt to improve their lives physically.

The writer has made his case and now he is concluding his work with a laundry list of moral "do's and don'ts"—godly instructions for successful living. As he writes, perhaps he notices the shadows shifting on his page as the sun makes its way across the sky, or he sees the words before him dance as the soft light from an oil lamp flickers in the breeze from the window.

And, all at once, in the middle of his practical advice, he feels compelled to insert a stunning affirmation. The words are Greek, but the English translation is simple: "Jesus Christ, yesterday and today, the same." And then, almost as an afterthought, he continues: "and unto the ages!"

The words are like a bolt of lightning, splitting the darkness and the silence without warning—and then, back to the good, solid advice.

But you don't forget the lightning. The image is seared in your mind. The sound continues to reverberate in your hearing: "Jesus Christ, the same. Yesterday and today, the same. Forever, the same."

So forget the good advice for a moment; forget the argument the writer so carefully crafted. Let the lightning startle you—stun you with its sudden and unexpected power. Let it scare you a little and dazzle you with the light that outshines everything else. Can you see it? Simple and spectacular: *"Jesus Christ, the same yesterday, today and forever!"*

෨෧

In my youth, a famous folk singer announced to the world that "the times they are a-changin'."[142] And so they were. But it wasn't like this was a revelation of something new—at least not for anybody who's been around for any length of time. The times are always changing. That's what times do. They're changing now. You can't stop it. You can't do much to control it.

And it's not just the times. Everything is changing. Every day, the world you know is passing away and a new one is forming right before your eyes. Things and people you know and love slip from your grasp.

You are changing. You woke up this morning, another day older, for sure, and, quite possibly, deeper in debt as well.[143] Again, you can't stop the reality of change and there isn't that much you can really do to control it. And even if some of the change you

[142] Bob Dylan, "The Times They Are a-Changin'," 1963.
[143] See "Sixteen Tons," by Merle Travis, 1947.

experience is positive, much of it is not. And all change is hard on the system.

If only there was something solid you could hold on to in this sea of change. If only there was something—someone—that didn't change—that was the same, yesterday, today and forever.

☙❧

And KA-BOOM! Jesus Christ. Jesus Christ is the same, yesterday, today and forever.

"Yes, all right, that's what the Bible says. But what does it mean? And what difference is it going to make for me, whatever it means?"

Well, let's take that last question first. Jesus Christ being the same yesterday, today and forever is going to make all the difference in the world to you—all the difference—in the world, and beyond the world. In fact, it already has. You see, this world will pass away.

Jesus said, *"Heaven and earth will pass away."*[144] But don't take God's word for it. Every atheist who is a reputable geologist, botanist, or astronomer agrees with God on that much.

And you and I and everyone else will pass away, too. We will pass away before this world does, unless God decides to intervene and send Jesus back in the near future. (About this divine intervention option, the atheist crowd is significantly less confident. But no matter.)

If Jesus Christ is going to be around "forever"—*"unto the ages,"* as the writer wrote it—He is going to be—and, in fact, already is—beyond the reach of this world and the changing times of this world. He is not subject to its changes. Nothing here that changes us, changes Him. Nothing here that prevents us from stopping or controlling change, or its impact on us, has any effect on Him.

---

[144] Mark 13:31, RSV.

Jesus Christ is the only Person you know Who could make a difference where it ultimately counts for you. And if He can—and if He will—well, that makes all the difference in the world.

❧

"But what does it mean for Jesus Christ to be the same yesterday, today and forever?"

It means the more things change, the more He stays the same. And that's true whether the writer had eternity past or the earthly ministry of Jesus in mind when he wrote the word "yesterday."

Because he wrote "*Jesus* Christ," I tend to think he was thinking of the time that Jesus spent teaching and preaching, healing and dying—those precious days in which God revealed Himself in the flesh—divinity among us.

There was barely a lifetime between the "yesterday" of Jesus in the flesh and the "today" of the writer of Hebrews. Yet even that short span of time had been long enough for many who would change the words of Jesus and the mission of Jesus and the person of Jesus into something other than what His disciples had discovered during that sacred and unique "yesterday."

Our "today" is thousands of years removed from that "yesterday," and legions of friends and enemies alike have reconfigured the idea of Jesus across those years to the point that now, some images of Him bear no resemblance to the portrait provided by the Gospels.

You could look at the vastly altered images of Jesus peddled today and despair. But the image or the idea is not the reality. The Person is!

No matter how many "Jesuses" we invent, the real Jesus Christ has never changed from the day He was conceived—from the day He began His ministry at the Jordan—from the day He healed the sick and fed the hungry and went to the Cross to pay the price for our sins and secure our salvation.

Right now, He is the same Jesus He was then. He is the same perfect and complete Expression of God's love for you. He is the same Pioneer of your faith.[145] He is the same Intercessor on your behalf with the heavenly Father.[146] He is the same Teacher of divine Truth.[147] He is the same only Way to the Father.[148]

He is the same Jesus Christ. Who He is—with you and for you—is exactly Who He was with and for Peter and James and John and Paul and Timothy—and the writer who penned those simple words not too many years later. You get the same exact Jesus they got.

You get the same Jesus Christ, today—and tomorrow—and the next day—and the day after that—and...

You "get the picture": Jesus Christ—the real Jesus Christ—the unchanged, the unchanging, the unchangeable Jesus Christ, every day of your ever-changing life in this ever-changing world. Then and now—the *same* Jesus Christ.

ॐ

The same Jesus Christ—but not just then and now. Jesus Christ is the same yesterday, today—and forever. Forever! *"Lo, I am with you always—even unto the end of the world.*[149] And I am still the same Jesus I've always been. I will always be the same Jesus I've always been."

KA-BOOM!

Martin Luther saw the lightning and his life was never the same.[150] And then he put pen to paper like that other writer and made some "lightning" of his own,

---

[145] Hebrews 2:10; 12:2.
[146] Romans 8:34; Hebrews 7:22-25.
[147] John 8:40.
[148] John 14:6.
[149] Matthew 28:20, KJV.
[150] On July 2, 1505, Luther was caught in a thunderstorm and was so frightened by it that he made a vow to become a monk if he was not struck by lightning.

"Did we in our own strength confide,
our striving would be losing.
Were not the right Man on our side,
the Man of God's own choosing.
Dost ask Who that may be?
Christ Jesus, it is He;
Lord Sabaoth, His name,
from age to age the same,
and He must win the battle."[151]

❦

"From age to age the same!"

What does that mean?

Another writer, the writer of Ecclesiastes, says, *"Everything the Lord does will endure forever."* [152] That means, according to the Psalmist, God's *righteousness* endures forever and His *love* endures forever and His *faithfulness* endures forever and His *plans* endure forever, which means He remembers His *covenant* forever,[153] and therefore, as Isaiah says, *"His salvation will last forever."*[154]

He will always be Jesus Christ—the same Jesus Christ Who came to this earth as a Baby born of woman to grow up and become the sacrificial Lamb

"...for a world of lost sinners...slain."[155]

This same Jesus Christ is your personal Savior today, not some modern myth or modified Messiah made more palatable by adapting Him to contemporary concepts of what He ought to be.

He survived the storm and kept the vow. See Carter Lindberg, *The European Reformations,* John Wiley & Sons: Oxford, UK, 2010, p. 61.
[151] Martin Luther, "A Mighty Fortress is Our God," 1529, English Translation, Frederick H. Hedge, 1852.
[152] Ecclesiastes 3:14, NIV.
[153] Psalms 111:3; 100:5; 117:2; 33:11; 105:8.
[154] Isaiah 51:6, NIV.
[155] See the hymn, "The Old Rugged Cross," George Bennard, 1913.

He is the same Jesus Christ Who is totally unfazed by current criticism and scholarly skepticism.

The real Jesus is the same Jesus Who was exactly Who God wanted Him to be,[156] despite every human and demonic effort to change Him[157]—the same Jesus Who was raised from the dead by the power of God to reign over everything on earth and in heaven, forever and ever.[158]

The times they are a-changin', all right. Thirty years after that song became the anthem for social protest and cultural transformation, it was being used as an advertising jingle for banks and accounting firms.[159] The times they are a-changing, but Jesus Christ is not.

FLASH!

Jesus Christ is the same yesterday, today and forever. Halleluiah! AMEN.

శ్రీ

---

[156] Mark 1:11.
[157] Matthew 4:1-11; 16:22-23.
[158] Revelation 11:15.
[159] In 1994, the song was used in TV commercials for the auditing and accountancy firm, Coopers & Lybrand; in 1996, in commercials for Canada's Bank of Montreal; and in 2005, in commercials for the insurance company, Kaiser Permanente.

From the Letter of James

James 1:17-27 NRSV

¹⁷ *Every generous act of giving, with every perfect gift, is from above, coming down from the Father of lights, with whom there is no variation or shadow due to change.* ¹⁸ *In fulfillment of his own purpose he gave us birth by the word of truth, so that we would become a kind of first fruits of his creatures.*

¹⁹ *You must understand this, my beloved: let everyone be quick to listen, slow to speak, slow to anger;* ²⁰ *for your anger does not produce God's righteousness.* ²¹ *Therefore rid yourselves of all sordidness and rank growth of wickedness, and welcome with meekness the implanted word that has the power to save your souls.*

²² *But be doers of the word, and not merely hearers who deceive themselves.* ²³ *For if any are hearers of the word and not doers, they are like those who look at themselves in a mirror;* ²⁴ *for they look at themselves and, on going away, immediately forget what they were like.* ²⁵ *But those who look into the perfect law, the law of liberty, and persevere, being not hearers who forget but doers who act—they will be blessed in their doing.*

²⁶ *If any think they are religious, and do not bridle their tongues but deceive their hearts, their religion is worthless.* ²⁷ *Religion that is pure and undefiled before God, the Father, is this: to care for orphans and widows in their distress, and to keep oneself unstained by the world.*

৵৽

27.

Practical Christianity

James 1:17-27 NRSV

There is a tired old line that preachers have used, probably for centuries, to describe the purpose of preaching. We say our job is to "comfort the afflicted and afflict the comfortable." You probably came today hoping for the comfort.

Well, don't hold your breath. The Epistle of James is just full of "afflict the comfortable," and, as is our custom here, we will play the scripture where it lies.

James starts out with the comfortable stuff: *"Every good gift and every perfect gift is from above, coming down from the Father of lights."*[160] Sounds almost like poetry. And this Heavenly Father gave us the ultimate good and perfect gift when He gave us birth by the word of truth. The word of truth is the gospel of Jesus Christ and the birth God gave us through it is the same spiritual re-birth Jesus told Nicodemus about in the Gospel of John.[161] We heard the good news and believed it and now we are new—born again in Jesus Christ.[162]

---

[160] James 1:17, KJV.
[161] John 3:1-8.
[162] 1 Peter 1:23.

This was not a whim on the part of God. This was not some spontaneous impulse. James says God made a deliberate, resolute decision to send His word of truth to us and let us hear this word of truth and transform us through our hearing of it—all to fulfill His purpose.

But there's a problem.

"Faith comes by hearing,"[163] says the Apostle Paul. But hearing is only the beginning of God's process, not the end of it. And there are Christians who are not seeing the process through to the end. Some people who have had the soul-saving word implanted within them are bailing out early on God when they've gotten what they want or all they think they need. They hang with the program until they peg out their "comfortable" meter, and from then on, as far as they're concerned, they're done.

James says, "This won't do. *Be doers of the word, and not merely hearers...."*

Hearing is comfortable. Hearing is pleasant—satisfying. Hearing can be inspirational. Everybody likes hearing God's word of salvation and blessing—God's word of truth. Hearing is good.

But hearing by itself is not good. The word of truth we hear tells us what God has done and is doing, in us, and for us. But that same word also tells us what we are to do in response to what God has done. The word of God is comfort; but it is also command.

"Oh, why don't you just 'tell me the stories of Jesus I long to hear'?"[164]

All right. Jesus said, *"Whoever has my commands and obeys them, he is the one who loves me."*[165]

Jesus said, *"There was a man who had two sons. He went to the first and said, 'Son, go and work today in the vineyard.'*

"'I will not,' he answered, but later he changed his mind and went.

Then the father went to the other son and said the same thing.

---

[163] Romans 10:17, KJV.
[164] See the hymn, "Tell Me the Stories of Jesus," William H. Parker, 1885.
[165] John 14:21, NIV.

"The son answered, 'I will, sir,' but he did not go."
And Jesus asked, *"Which of the two did what his father wanted?"*[166]

৵৹

Hearing and doing—according to Jesus.

To hear the word of truth and not do the word of truth is not merely disobedient, it is self-deceiving. Just because you are satisfied with the intellectual and emotional stimulation that religious activity—such as scripture reading and sermon hearing—provides you, you should not assume that God is satisfied, too.

James makes very clear that God is not at all satisfied when we sit back and passively absorb the gracious gift contained in His holy word and do nothing in response. Just as God had a purpose in transforming us through the power of His word to begin with, He also has a clearly defined, divine purpose every time He speaks to us—through His words of the Bible, or through any aspect of our worship and study that lifts up or illuminates His word.

To hear the word without responding with action is a useless expenditure of time. You hear and then you walk away, leaving what you heard like your reflection in a mirror when you step away from it: The point and power of the word disappear as quickly and completely as your image does.

You hear the word of God to stimulate your mind or warm your heart, but if you do not act on your insight or out of your joy and gratitude, it has all been wasted, because it has all been about *you.* And because the word of truth is never ultimately about any one of us, you will misappropriate the wisdom and power and grace of God's word if what you hear remains sealed up inside you and not acted upon appropriately.

Are you feeling adequately afflicted?

Me, too.

---

[166] Matthew 21:28-31, NIV.

Fortunately, this is not the last word. James' purpose is not merely to afflict comfortable, hearing-only hearers. It is to motivate and inspire *"doing* hearers"—in other words, Christians who hear God's word of truth and then *do* what God's word tells them to do.

Those who are determined to be hearers *and* doers of the word will act. And, according to James, they will be blessed for doing so. Not because they act, per se. Doing without hearing is as bad as hearing without doing.

They will be blessed because they act upon the word of truth they hear. They look into *"the perfect law of liberty"* (another way of saying God's word of truth) and they focus on it continuously. They listen to the word—they look into the perfect law—with a persevering commitment to both hear and do, which is totally different from the fleeting-glance approach of those who are content with the comfortable experience of uninvolved observation.

❧

But what are you to do, as a hearer of the word, when you have determined that you will *do* as well as hear? The Bible is full of things to do (and things we are *not* to do, as some like to point out).

James boils it down to two things—two things that you are to do if your religion is to be pure and undefiled before God—two things for doers of the word: Care for orphans and widows in their distress and keep yourself unstained by the world.

Before you get too comfortable with this list, you need to realize that the list is suggestive—not all-inclusive. James is giving a single and colorful example for each of two broad and basic categories. It's kind of like when Jesus says, "Love the Lord your God with all your heart, soul, mind and strength and your neighbor as yourself."[167]

---

[167] Luke 10:27.

Do you see the similarity? What we are to do when we "hear the word" falls into two categories: things we do in our relationship to God and things we do in our relationship to others?

Let's boil it down a little more: the two categories for Christian action are personal morality and social morality.

Personal morality means keeping yourself unstained by the world. The word for "unstained" is the same word for designating an animal worthy for sacrifice:[168] without spot or blemish,[169] and, therefore, acceptable as an offering to God. The hearer of the word must do all those things that prevent him or her being tainted and tarnished by the evils of a very tempting world.

Social morality is summed up in the command to care for orphans and widows in their distress. Socially and economically, these were the weakest and the most vulnerable in the community. The word for their "distress" is the word used elsewhere the New Testament for "tribulation"[170] and "affliction."[171] It is the word used to describe what Christians suffered for Christ.[172] Hearers of the word are to do what Christ did for the helpless in society to alleviate their personal tribulations.

But here is an interesting thing. Even if we are inclined to be doers of the word, most of us are still inclined to do our "doing" in only one of these categories, not both.

If you are conservative by nature, you are more likely to emphasize personal morality—to devote yourself to behaviors that avoid personal vices—to promote character and integrity. You are more likely to grow weary or frustrated with programs of social betterment and the people promoting or profiting by them.

On the other hand, if you are of a liberal point of view, you may see feeding, clothing, housing and healing society's under-

---

[168] Leviticus 1:3.
[169] Ephesians 5:27.
[170] John 16:22.
[171] 2 Corinthians 1:4.
[172] Matthew 24:9; Colossians 1:24.

privileged as God's top priority for doers of the word. Public policy and compassionate social causes trump personal moral behavior, which may seem presumptuous to address in others and tedious to observe in your own life.

Are these stereotypes?

Yes, but not without precedent, and useful as general concepts to point out that doers of the word are directed to do both—to live with, and promote, personal morality—*and* to improve the lot of those in need—if we are to be pure and undefiled before God. The liberal is to be conservative in his commitment to personal morality, and the conservative is to be liberal in his ministry to those who are suffering.

May I bring Paul back into the discussion for a minute? People think Paul and James are worlds apart, but they're not, really. Paul says, *"we have not stopped praying for you and asking God to fill you with the knowledge of his will through all spiritual wisdom and understanding."* [173] (Do you hear it: *"...fill you with the knowledge of his will"? "Be hearers of the word"?*)

And Paul goes on: *"And we pray this in order that you may live a life worthy of the Lord and may please him in every way: bearing fruit in every good work..."* [174] (And there's the rest of it: *"...bearing fruit in every good work..." "...be doers of the word."*)

Hearing and doing God's word of truth, personally and socially...

Can you get comfortable with that?

৯ৼৡ

---

[173] Colossians 1:9, NIV.
[174] Colossians 1:10, NIV.

James 2:1-13 NRSV

 ¹ *My brothers and sisters, do you with your acts of favoritism really believe in our glorious Lord Jesus Christ? ² For if a person with gold rings and in fine clothes comes into your assembly, and if a poor person in dirty clothes also comes in, ³ and if you take notice of the one wearing the fine clothes and say, "Have a seat here, please," while to the one who is poor you say, "Stand there," or, "Sit at my feet," ⁴ have you not made distinctions among yourselves, and become judges with evil thoughts? ⁵ Listen, my beloved brothers and sisters. Has not God chosen the poor in the world to be rich in faith and to be heirs of the kingdom that he has promised to those who love him? ⁶ But you have dishonored the poor. Is it not the rich who oppress you? Is it not they who drag you into court? ⁷ Is it not they who blaspheme the excellent name that was invoked over you?*

⁸ You do well if you really fulfill the royal law according to the scripture, "You shall love your neighbor as yourself." ⁹ But if you show partiality, you commit sin and are convicted by the law as transgressors. ¹⁰ For whoever keeps the whole law but fails in one point has become accountable for all of it. ¹¹ For the one who said, "You shall not commit adultery," also said, "You shall not murder." Now if you do not commit adultery but if you murder, you have become a transgressor of the law. ¹² So speak and so act as those who are to be judged by the law of liberty. ¹³ For judgment will be without mercy to anyone who has shown no mercy; mercy triumphs over judgment.

೨∾ఄ

28.

The Royal Law of Love

James 2:1-13 NRSV

Christianity would be a whole lot easier religion if there weren't so many other people involved. If it were just Jesus and you—wouldn't it be wonderful? You would be singing, "Every day with Jesus is sweeter than the day before."[175]

But, of course, every day isn't just with Jesus. Look around. Even at the early service, there are dozens of other people, and every one of them wants a bit of the Lord's time and attention, just like you do. There'll be hundreds more here before the day's over. Almost a thousand of us are members of this Chapel now—all loving Jesus and being loved by Him—all of them your brothers and sisters in Christ, according to the Bible.

You've got more brothers and sisters in other churches, millions of them around the world—all related to Jesus just like you are—loved by Jesus, just like you are. Loving Jesus is easy, but Jesus says you're supposed to love all these brothers and sisters, too.

And then there's everybody else—everybody else who isn't a Christian—and you're supposed to love them, too, because Jesus

---

[175] "Every Day with Jesus is Sweeter Than the Day Before," Robert Claire Loveless, 1936.

says—and the Old Testament before Him said—they're neighbors you're supposed to love as much as you love yourself.[176]

If you're a Christian, you're supposed to love strangers in the world and people you know in the church the same way you love yourself, and, interestingly enough, sometimes it's easier to love the strangers—because you don't know them. You can love them abstractly—in a generic, theoretical sort of way.

But you know people in the Chapel. You know what they're like—what they think—what they do. You know that some of them are more lovable than others. You know how they're different from each other—and which of the differences you like better. And that's part of what makes Christianity harder than you want it to be.

The Bible says—James says to us today—that God is no respecter of persons and that you as His child in Christ are not allowed to favor one of your spiritual siblings over another, however much you want to.

As usual, James paints an uncomfortable picture to make a point. But in this case, it is also a confusing one—so let's study it a minute.

&⁊❧

Two men come into their assembly. One is wearing dazzling jewelry and a stunning outfit. The fingers of the second are encased in grime rather than gold, and the only thing stunning about his clothes is the foul smell they give off. James describes their reception by the church: The rich man gets the royal treatment; the poor man gets the bum's rush.

You have formed a mental image of the scene. Now let me mess with it.

If you are seeing a worship service like ours and two visitors coming in and being greeted in two different ways, think instead

---

[176] Luke 10:27; Leviticus 19:18.

of two members of the church who have a dispute and come before the leaders of the church who will judge between them and render a verdict.

In a corrupt world, where do you go for justice? Many who had become Christians went to their new spiritual brothers and sisters—because they trusted in them, because they trusted in Jesus.

The rich member is impressive. He can help the church financially—and with his network of contacts in business, society and government. The poor member can do nothing—except perhaps drive prospects away.

ॐॐॐ

But if the other members of the church show partiality—if they favor one or the other because of their perceived human value to the church—the church ceases to be the church.

For the church is the one place where every person is exactly the same in the only category that counts: Everybody in the church is a person who, though condemned by sin, has been redeemed by the all-powerful and sacrificial love of Jesus.

Christianity would be a whole lot easier religion if there weren't so many perceived differences involved. *Perceived* differences.

You want Christianity to be easier? You don't have to get rid of all the other people huddling around Jesus so you can have Him and love Him all by yourself. Just fulfill the royal law, as James calls it: Love them all as you love yourself.

If you do, every day with Jesus *will* be sweeter than the day before.

ॐॐॐ

James 3:1-12 NRSV

¹ Not many of you should become teachers, my brothers and sisters, for you know that we who teach will be judged with greater strictness. ² For all of us make many mistakes. Anyone who makes no mistakes in speaking is perfect, able to keep the whole body in check with a bridle. ³ If we put bits into the mouths of horses to make them obey us, we guide their whole bodies. ⁴ Or look at ships: though they are so large that it takes strong winds to drive them, yet they are guided by a very small rudder wherever the will of the pilot directs. ⁵ So also the tongue is a small member, yet it boasts of great exploits.

How great a forest is set ablaze by a small fire! ⁶ And the tongue is a fire. The tongue is placed among our members as a world of iniquity; it stains the whole body, sets on fire the cycle of nature, and is itself set on fire by hell. ⁷ For every species of beast and bird, of reptile and sea creature, can be tamed and has been tamed by the human species, ⁸ but no one can tame the tongue—a restless evil, full of deadly poison. ⁹ With it we bless the Lord and Father, and with it we curse those who are made in the likeness of God. ¹⁰ From the same mouth come blessing and cursing. My brothers and sisters, this ought not to be so. ¹¹ Does a spring pour forth from the same opening both fresh and brackish water? ¹² Can a fig tree, my brothers and sisters, yield olives, or a grapevine figs? No more can salt water yield fresh.

৵৽

29.

Mind Your Helm

James 3:1-12 NRSV

Have you ever said something you wanted to take back? And did you say, "I take it back." And did that work? Were you able to take back what you said?

No, it doesn't really work that way. When you speak, what you speak becomes real—it takes on a life of its own. You can say something else about it—you can do something to try and mitigate the impact of what you said—but your words and their meaning have been "created" as surely as God created the world by speaking it into existence.[177]

What you say will not last forever, but it will last as long as everybody who hears it—and everybody who is told about it—remembers it. And that can still be a very long time.

But you know all this—if you ever said something you wanted to take back. And if you haven't, you probably will. James says, *"Anyone who makes no mistakes in speaking is perfect."* And what he doesn't say (because he figures you know it already, too), is that nobody but Jesus is perfect, which means Jesus is the only One Who's never made a mistake in speaking.

---

[177] Genesis 1.

So where does that leave the rest of us? It leaves us with untamed tongues, according to James—tongues that stain the whole person with iniquity—tongues that start trouble like a match starts a forest fire—tongues that seem to know just how to sting like the bite of a poisonous snake. James doesn't sugarcoat it: Hell comes out of our mouths because hell gets into our hearts.

For some of us, it happens all the time—every time we open our mouths, so to speak. For others, it's once in a blue moon. For some, it's brash and blatant, cussin' and swearin' like a verbal cesspool. For others, it is the ever so soft and subtle incision into someone's character or motives. Evil words can be premeditated or impulsive. Either way, they are still evil.

Whatever the form or frequency, the potential for evil is always there because the tongue is always there—along with all the mental and emotional apparatus inside us that sets the toxic tongue in motion.

Children are abused by the toxic tongues of their parents. And, increasingly, parents are abused by the toxic tongues of their children, both young and old. Spouses say evil things to each other they would not say to a stranger. Employers belittle their employees, and, when those employers are not around, the workers criticize them in return.

We will not even get into the nature of political debate today, but we will say that even Christians are not above turning their evil words on other Christians. To borrow a dramatic word from James, *"My brothers and sisters, this ought not be so!"*

"But I meant no harm."

Do not say that you "meant no harm" when you know how harmful words can be and you took no precaution to protect other people from yours.

"I just said what was on my heart."

And if what you said was evil, who let it into your heart? Does wanting to speak make what you say right? And even if what you say may be right *in content*—is it right that you convey it in the setting and in the manner and to the individuals you do?

"I've got a right to say what I want to—'freedom of speech,' you know."

Do you think Almighty God will let you hide behind America's Bill of Rights when you stand before Him in Judgment? You won't be an American anymore then.

Jesus said, *"I tell you that men will have to give account on the day of judgment for every careless word they have spoken. For by your words you will be acquitted, and by your words you will be condemned."*[178]

And, by the way, I submit to you that the founders of this country confirmed the right to speak not so that people could say whatever they felt like saying, but so that anyone could safely say those unpopular things that need to be said for the good of the country and its citizens. To abuse that freedom for personal ego gratification or other evil purpose is to undermine the strength of that right—to tarnish its beauty and offend the God Who ultimately gave it and guards it.

But let's get back to the business of the toxic tongue. James takes no prisoners and grants no pardons. This is a hard business and James would have us face it head on. So let us confront some hard questions: Do you speak in ways that leave others in tears—or hopping mad? Do you damage reputations or undermine the work of the kingdom by sowing discord or discontent?

Where does your talk take you—closer to God or farther from Him? Where does it take (or drive) others—the people you talk to (or about)? Do your words lead others into sin of their own, permitting, by your speech, evil speech on their part that might have been defused by godly words from you?

You have heard every evil word you have ever said. More than anyone, you know what you say and how you say it. So ask yourself: "Where does the evil come out in my words? Where are the weak

---

[178] Matthew 12:36-37, NIV.

spots in my 'verbal containment field'? What can I do to bridle my tongue as James urges me to?"

James uses the analogy of a rider whose hold on the bridle controls the whole horse. But James uses another image that may be even more apropos—and useful: a nautical image. "Look at ships," he says.

In James' day, an average sized merchant ship carried two or three hundred tons of cargo and might be 200 feet long. Today, merchant ships carry 400 times as much cargo and are a thousand feet longer. Today, ships are driven by powerful engines, burning oil or gas. James would have seen ships driven by the wind. But one thing is the same, then as now: Great ships are guided by a rudder that is ridiculously small compared to the ship whose destiny it directs.

But, of course, the rudder that controls the great ship must itself be controlled, or it becomes an instrument of destruction. Ships of the ancient world were steered by a tiller attached to the rudder. Today, the rudder is controlled by a helm—a wheel connected to the rudder by ropes and gears and mounted high in the control center of the ship.

And what are we to learn from this image that will help us control the toxic tongue—the "rudder" of the ship of our lives? The rudder can alter the course of the ship and direct it to safety, when the rudder is controlled properly. An uncontrolled rudder can—will—take you to the wrong destination—at best. At worst, it could sink the ship. "Loose lips sink ships"[179] in more than one way.

What you may not realize if you are watching a ship from the shore—but will certainly see if you observe the ship at sea—is this: You cannot tell your course in the midst of the ocean with its lack of fixed landmarks amid the chaos of wind and wave. The ocean is trackless.

---

[179] From the U. S. War Advertising Council during World War II.

You must focus on the compass that always points the way—the compass available to everyone who takes the helm to control the rudder and steer the ship. But just having a compass will not guarantee that the helm will control the rudder sufficiently to bring the ship to the proper port.

The helm must be held tightly—meticulously—on course by the helmsman. The helmsman must fix his attention on the compass and ignore everything else going on around him. He must constantly point the rudder controlling the ship straight at the proper point on the compass—moment by moment—hour after hour—come what may in the sea before him and the ship around him.

And if the helmsman does not do this—if the one who holds the wheel in his hands and controls the rudder that directs the ship does not keep the ship on course—then the one who set the course, the pilot, will say to him, "Mind your helm. You are not paying enough attention to your one essential task: controlling the rudder. You have allowed the rudder to take the ship where it wants to go instead of where I would have it go. Refocus your attention on the compass and steer the ship accordingly."

And when the helmsman does as the pilot orders, the ship returns to its proper course.

In the Navy Chapel at the Little Creek Amphibious Base in Virginia, there is a beautiful stained-glass window. Pictured in the window is a young sailor, manning the helm of his ship on a dark night in a raging storm. Behind him stands a loving and determined Jesus, Whose strong hands have also grasped the helm—Whose eyes are fixed on their compass, and beyond it to the safe harbor that awaits them on the other side of the storm. Together, they will maintain the course—the course their divine Pilot had set. It is a beautiful picture of God's strong protection, and it will serve James' purpose as well to show us that we must—and can—control our tongues—the rudder of our ship.

How can a little rudder control a great ship? How can you and I control the untamable tongue?

Only as we accept the assignment to "mind our helm" and make room for Christ to add His strength to our own can we succeed where we will always otherwise fail. Only when we allow Jesus, the one perfect Man, to take a hand in controlling what we cannot—the evil we think and speak—will we be able to pray without hypocrisy:

"Let the words of my mouth and the meditations of my heart be acceptable in Thy sight, O Lord, my Strength and my Redeemer. Amen."[180]

ॐ

---

[180] It was my practice to pray this slightly altered verse from the King James Version of Psalm 19:14 before I began to preach a sermon.

From the First Letter of Peter

30.

Not Seeing and True Believing

1 Peter 1:3-9 RSV

Forty-one years ago, I was invited to serve as Youth Minister here during my summer break from seminary.[181] The following year, I came back and married a woman I had met here, in the old sanctuary—the room where your early service now meets.

Thirty years ago, that wife and I and our daughter became members here, when a Navy assignment brought us back to the area. It was here that our daughter made her profession of faith.

I am glad today to be back again in a church with so many good memories for us.

Several weeks ago, I was flipping through some old sermon notebooks and came across a sermon I had written during my first summer here. In fact, it must have been the first sermon I ever wrote.

I never actually got to preach it here. And because of the compassion and respect I feel for you, I will not preach it today, either.

---

[181] After retiring from full-time pastoral ministry, my wife and I returned to the Tidewater Virginia area. Several months later, I was asked to "fill in" for a few Sundays in the church where so many important events in my life had occurred.

Today, I want to share with you what somebody else wrote—not a young, inexperienced, student preacher, but an old, well-seasoned warrior of the Christian faith who witnessed the Resurrection of Jesus Christ and was at the forefront of the founding of the Church. And as I read what he wrote, I would like for you to imagine that *you* are the church that he is writing to—that *you* are the Christians the great Simon Peter has taken the time to encourage and instruct.

Before it became part of the Bible, Peter's letter was just that: a letter to groups of Christians who had formed themselves into churches. And because the letter *was* included in the New Testament, what Peter wrote those churches has become his letter to all churches—including yours.

What you are about to hear is from the first chapter of Peter's first letter, beginning with verse 3.

৯৯৩

³ Blessed be the God and Father of our Lord Jesus Christ!

By His great mercy we have been born anew to a living hope through the resurrection of Jesus Christ from the dead, ⁴ and to an inheritance which is imperishable, undefiled, and unfading, kept in heaven for you, ⁵ who, by God's power, are guarded through faith for a salvation ready to be revealed in the last time.

⁶ In this you rejoice, though now for a little while, you may have to suffer various trials, ⁷ so that the genuineness of your faith, more precious than gold which, though perishable, is tested by fire, may redound to praise and glory and honor at the revelation of Jesus Christ.

⁸ Without having seen Him, you love Him; though you do not now see Him, you believe in Him, and rejoice with unutterable and exalted joy. ⁹ As the outcome of your faith, you obtain the salvation of your souls.

৯৯৩

Did you notice that the first thing Peter says in his letter to you—is not directed to *you*?

It's directed to God: *"Blessed be the God and Father of our Lord Jesus Christ!"*

It's as though Peter assumes that when his letter is read to you, God will be here listening, too. Is that something *you* assume, as you hear what is said and see what is done in the worship service each week? As you look around to see who made it to church, do you see the One Who is unseen by human eyes—Who never misses a Sunday with you?

Make a note for future reference: God is always here.

The first thing Peter writes in his letter proper—that he knows will be read in church—to the body of believers gathered in worship—is *worship*—joyful, full-throated praise to God. It's like the Doxology we used to sing in my home church every Sunday when I was growing up: "Praise God from Whom all blessings flow!" and so forth. The focus on God is where true worship begins.

So, yes, *"Blessed be the God and Father of our Lord Jesus Christ!"*

And now, let's find out why.

෨⊷෨

Why is God so worthy of your praise?

And to make it more personal, Peter puts the answer in the first-person plural: *we.* "You and I—," he says, "all of us Christians—have a living hope and a heavenly inheritance—from God." That's why Peter starts out with praise and worship.

Last week, you celebrated Easter. But the Resurrection is not a one-Sunday blip on the religious radar screen. For someone who was "there" when it happened, the emotional and psychological impact of the experience probably doesn't wear off quickly—or at all. And what Peter is telling you is that the functional impact of God's raising of Jesus Christ for *you* will never wear off, either.

The gospel—the story of the Resurrection and everything that goes with it—is good news because it has overcome all the bad news that was messing up everything before the good news came along.[182] Through the Resurrection, you *"have been born anew to a living hope"*—which is good news, because before that, you didn't have any hope—any real hope—which is very bad news.

Through the Resurrection, you have come into an incredible inheritance—which is good news, because as far as eternity is concerned, before the Resurrection, you had nothing. You were dead broke spiritually—and worse: guilty as sin without a penny to pay the fine, except that you can't pay this fine in money, even if you have all the money in the world! This fine is paid in blood—and eternal suffering—which, again, is very bad news.

And now, you don't have to pay your fine. Now, you are eternally rich in every kind of eternally wonderful stuff. Now, you're not just waiting for this life to be over and trying to avoid as much of the bad parts of it as possible in the meantime. Now, your life here means something wonderful because it is an inseparable part of something that will culminate in "complete and eternal wonderful-ness." And all of this has been made possible, Peter writes you, because of what God did in raising Jesus Christ from the dead.

Whatever is going on in your life right now, it is part of the new life God has given you for eternity, which means that the *meaning* of whatever is going on in your life in the present—as well as what went on in the past—and what will go on in the future— is already and always *defined* by what will ultimately become of your life for all eternity—which will be unimaginably and infinitely good.

This "living" hope is now the "world"—the "environment"— of your consciousness and experience because you have been "born into it" spiritually, as truly and completely as you were born physically into this physical world. We Christians live in a divine reality that is only available to those who believe in the Resurrection and the message of Jesus that it validates.

---

[182] See Frederick Buechner, *Telling the Truth: The Gospel as Tragedy, Comedy and Fairy Tale*, Harper & Row, 1977, p. 7.

For those who don't believe, this whole divine reality doesn't exist. *It's* there, but *they're* not. So be careful when dealing with them, because they don't know everything you know. They don't live in the reality you live in. They don't have access to the blessings and the power and the hope that you do—as long as they choose *not* to believe in the Source of the hope and inheritance that has been given freely to you.

৵৽

Given freely.

You don't deserve the hope *or* the inheritance that God has given us freely. Neither do I. And neither, for that matter, does Simon Peter. In remembering his encounter with the Risen Christ on that first Easter Sunday, he also remembers the night, several days before, when a rooster crowed to cut into his foul-mouthed denials of the Jesus he had promised so proudly and publicly to die for.

And so, *"Blessed be the God and Father of our Lord Jesus Christ"* for His great mercy in giving us what we had to have—and could not get ourselves.

And *"Blessed be God"* for His power guarding our inheritance of salvation, in heaven, until it is revealed to the world and delivered to us when Jesus comes back for us. There's an image for you: God as the Guard over your salvation—your inheritance that He is keeping imperishable, undefiled and unfading in heaven.

Have you seen the commercials recently about the uniformed fellow in a bank watching indifferently, placidly, as a gang of thieves stage a hold-up? That's *not* the way God guards our most important possession.

I sometimes lose track of where I placed important papers for safekeeping, having no idea where I put them when I go to find them. *That's* not the way God guards our most important possession, either.

Or for that matter, says Peter, how God guards *us*.

Your inheritance is not the only thing God is guarding. God is also guarding you: *"...by God's power [you] are guarded through faith for ...salvation."*

The faith you have exercised by believing in Jesus Christ was a gift that God gave you to use for your salvation. And you have used it. God has given that gift to everyone, though many refuse to use it, and others simply don't know how.

But your faith itself is a shield of protection God has placed around you that keeps you in His care every moment, so that you will be ready and qualified to receive the fullness of your eternal salvation at the proper time. As I said earlier, God is always here with you when you worship. And here, Peter goes further to say that God is always with you *everywhere*, to protect you.

❧❦

"But what about all the hassles and hardships I have to put up with every day?!"

Peter doesn't deny that you *"have to suffer various trials,"* though he's primarily pointing to the harassment other people direct at you because of your faith and how your faith plays out in practical ways around them. Still, life is often no picnic, no matter how much time, talent and treasure you put into the practice of your faith.

So how do you maintain hope and happiness in the face of hard times and heartbreak?

According to Peter, by recognizing that your suffering as a Christian is not meaningless like the suffering of others may be. All you endure in your faith is a testing and refinement of your faith so that you are drawn deeper in faith and closer to Christ in the process—that your suffering, sanctified and transformed in the loving hands of God, becomes the gifts of understanding, compassion, strength and encouragement that God gives *through* you to others to redeem *their* suffering.

We will not praise God for the pain we endure now, writes Peter, but we will praise Him for what He does with our pain, which He can only do through our faith, because we believe that He can and will redeem everything we go through in this life. And we will praise God most of all in the end when He gives us the spiritual eyes to see the full picture of what He did with our suffering—in us and in others.

ॐ◦ॐ

"Oh, if I only had a faith like Peter's to believe that!"

Well, here's an interesting thing: Peter is more impressed with *your* faith than he is with his own. To him, *you* have more faith than he does. He marvels that *"Without having seen him, you love him; though you do not now see him, you believe in him…"*

Peter was *"there."* He saw it all—up close and personal! He almost *has to* believe. How can he *not?*

But you didn't go through the same "basic training" he did, and you still joined up and lined up next to him and James and John and Paul and all the other famous folks in the ranks of the faithful you read about in the Bible.

You love Jesus. You believe in Him. You rejoice with incredible joy because of Him. And you haven't even *seen* Him the way Peter and the rest of them did.

Yours is the stronger faith! And don't let anybody tell you different. I almost called this sermon, *"Not* Seeing is Believing." That seems to be what Peter is saying.

Jesus said the same thing when Thomas finally got a chance to see His Risen Lord after the Resurrection: "Well, Thomas, you've seen Me, and now you believe what the rest of them were telling you about Me. And that's good. But those who won't have the benefit of seeing Me 'in the (risen) flesh' and believe anyway—*those* will be the true giants of faith."

"But my faith isn't that strong!"

Is it "faith" if you never have any trouble holding on to it?

The point is that you do hold on to it, hard as it is to do so in the hard times. And that's what makes it faith. Strengthen your faith as best you can, with God's help, in good times and bad, but know that as long as you have it—in whatever shape it's in—you have the living hope God has given you and the heavenly inheritance God guards for you. Faith in the trenches does not wear a parade-ground uniform.

"Blessed be the God and Father of our Lord Jesus Christ!" writes Peter.

"Blessed are those who have not seen and yet believed," said the Risen Christ to His disciples.[183]

God is here—watching—listening—we've said.

Anybody here ready to believe—to put your faith in Jesus?

೧⊷ଓ

---

[183] John 20:27.

1 Peter 2:1-10 ESV

¹ *So put away all malice and all deceit and hypocrisy and envy and all slander.* ² *Like newborn infants, long for the pure spiritual milk, that by it you may grow up into salvation—* ³ *if indeed you have tasted that the Lord is good.*

⁴ *As you come to him, a living stone rejected by men but in the sight of God chosen and precious,* ⁵ *you yourselves like living stones are being built up as a spiritual house, to be a holy priesthood, to offer spiritual sacrifices acceptable to God through Jesus Christ.* ⁶ *For it stands in Scripture:*

> *"Behold, I am laying in Zion a stone,*
> *a cornerstone chosen and precious,*
> *and whoever believes in him*
> *will not be put to shame."*

⁷ *So the honor is for you who believe, but for those who do not believe,*

> *"The stone that the builders rejected*
> *has become the cornerstone,"*

⁸ *and*

> *"A stone of stumbling,*
> *and a rock of offense."*

They stumble because they disobey the word, as they were destined to do.

⁹ *But you are a chosen race, a royal priesthood, a holy nation, a people for his own possession, that you may proclaim the excellencies of him who called you out of darkness into his marvelous light.* ¹⁰ *Once you were not a people, but now you are God's people; once you had not received mercy, but now you have received mercy.*

⫷∞⫸

John 15:12-16 ESV

[Jesus said:]

¹² *"This is my commandment, that you love one another as I have loved you. ¹³ Greater love has no one than this, that someone lay down his life for his friends. ¹⁴ You are my friends if you do what I command you. ¹⁵ No longer do I call you servants, for the servant does not know what his master is doing; but I have called you friends, for all that I have heard from my Father I have made known to you. ¹⁶ You did not choose me, but I chose you and appointed you that you should go and bear fruit and that your fruit should abide, so that whatever you ask the Father in my name, he may give it to you. ¹⁷ These things I command you, so that you will love one another."*

❧

31.

Who Do You Think You Are?

1 Peter 2:1-10; John 15:12-16 ESV

I am occasionally criticized—gently and lovingly—for not including enough "practical application" in my sermons. I plead guilty. I do not often tell you, "The Bible says, 'Do this' or 'Do that.'" I try to help you understand the gospel revealed in the pages of the Bible, believing that, with that understanding, you will then make the practical applications appropriate to you and your circumstances.

☙◦❧

Today is different. The sermon you are about to hear is intended for *immediate* application. I want to tell you what the Bible says you are to do—and not do—in the membership meeting we will convene at the conclusion of this service. So if you are visiting with us today, you get a pass; I am talking to the voting members of this particular congregation.

Beloved, I do not intend to tell you how to vote on the matter our Church Council will bring to you for your consideration. *What* we decide is far less important—for the future of our church and in the eyes of God—than *how* we decide. A right decision made the wrong way is far worse than a wrong decision reached the right way.

And lest you think I am going to take unfair advantage of my pulpit privileges to pound you with some personal agenda, I assure you that I have not stacked the deck, biblically, today, by picking a passage at the last minute that would let me "get something off my chest." Today's passages in First Peter and John's Gospel were selected a year ago for this date, as part of an almost three-year-long project of preaching through the Bible from Genesis to Revelation, a project asked for by many of you.

But sometimes, as you read a passage of scripture in preparation to preach it, you sense a divine purpose greater than any human plan—even a plan intended to edify and, hopefully, inspire. As I began to read and reflect on today's passages over the past few weeks, in the context of unfolding events in our church—and the attitudes and actions that have accompanied them—I came to suspect that God knew we would need to hear these sacred words today, and led me to put them on the preaching schedule many months ago—*"for such a time as this."*[184]

Several weeks ago, I told you that God will never tempt you, but the devil will. Well, the devil has been tempting us desperately of late, with some success. We stand on the verge of a great new chapter in our amazing story. We finally have a permanent facility. We see exciting possibilities ahead. We have much to do to make those possibilities realities. And we have many practical frustrations to endure until we do.

But with so much on our earthly agendas, we become susceptible to losing sight of the higher, spiritual things. As we focus on what we are doing—and what we think we ought to be doing—we run the risk of forgetting who we are.

And who are we?

---

[184] A famous line from Esther 4:4.

According to Peter, we *"are a chosen race, a royal priesthood, a holy nation, a people for God's own possession."*

Each of us was a sinner, condemned, by any measure of justice, to eternal damnation. Each of us was cut off from God and helpless to do anything about our dilemma except make it worse, if that were possible.[185] Jesus changed all that, for every one of us who put our faith in Him.[186]

But that's not all. When we were cut off from God, we were also cut off from everybody else, coming together with other people only to conspire in the pursuit of greater godlessness.

But what Jesus did on the Cross for each of us individually was only the beginning.[187] He did something remarkable with us collectively as well. We are, together, now, what the Bible claimed for the children of Israel as God brought them out of bondage in Egypt and led them through the desert to the Promised Land.[188]

We are, together, divinely chosen.[189] We are all "blood relatives" in that we are all God's cherished children,[190] intimately related by the shed Blood of His Son Jesus Christ.[191] The membership of this church, in total, is a royal priesthood. All of us together are authorized and required to mediate the grace of Jesus Christ to each other and all outside our fellowship who will receive it.[192]

Like an embassy in foreign territory, we are one small outpost of God's sacred soil, His sovereign nation, representing Him and serving His will in this world.[193] We are fellow citizens of heaven on temporary assignment here.[194]

---

[185] Ephesians 2:12.
[186] Romans 3:21-26.
[187] Ephesians 2:13-14.
[188] Deuteronomy 7:6.
[189] John 15:16.
[190] 1 John 1:3.
[191] Romans 6:5.
[192] 1 Corinthians 12:4-8; Ephesians 4:4-7.
[193] John 17:18.
[194] Philippians 3:20.

We are God's possession; God owns us, lock, stock and barrel.[195] We—all of us—together—*are* the church.[196] That is an eternal, universal reality infinitely greater and more important—at least to God—than anything else any one of us—or any group of us—may decide to assign some measure of importance to.

❧

So here's the practical application: After the benediction, we are all going to file out of this room, pick up a ballot outside and come back in here to hear what our Council Chairman has to say on behalf of the Council. Then, those of us who wish, may say what we want to say about the matter at hand. At some point, we will probably take a vote. If we do—and depending on what the majority decides—other actions will be set in motion in our church.

If we were merely a group of people with a group of opinions—and if our opinions were strongly held—we might be inclined to do or say just about anything to promote our preferred position or undermine positions we do not wish to see adopted. And our emotional reactions to comments—and the final result— might be satisfied or frustrated, happy or hostile. We might find ourselves polarized from those we disagree with, and more distant from God.

And the devil's temptation will have succeeded brilliantly.

But wherever there is devilish temptation, there is divine testing also.[197] There is the opportunity to overcome the temptation through a steadfastness of faith in which we are refined and strengthened individually and as a church body.[198]

Here's the test: Will we recognize, when we come back into this place—where we are now engaged in sacred worship—that we

---

[195] 1 Corinthians 6:19-20.
[196] Romans 12:4-5.
[197] 1 Corinthians 10:13.
[198] 1 Peter 1:22.

will not just be coming into a business meeting? Will we recognize that we will be coming back into the presence of the Risen Christ, our Savior and Lord?[199]

The business matter to be discussed and disposed of in some way will not be the primary issue on *God's* agenda. The true question God will be looking to see answered by us is this: Do we know that we, as a church, are *"living stones…being built up as a spiritual house, to be a holy priesthood, to offer spiritual sacrifices acceptable to God through Jesus Christ"*?

Here's a news flash: God doesn't care what we decide to do. There's no moral or spiritual essential involved today, except our self-understanding and our treatment of one another. If we get the vote wrong, God will work it out.[200] He's been redeeming our mistakes from the beginning, and there's nothing we can mess up so bad that God can't make it right.[201]

But if we do not come back into this place knowing who we really are, we run the risk of messing up "royally," because we are God's royal priesthood. And if we do not treat with honor and respect the Temple of the Holy Spirit that every single one of us helps to make up, we will abuse the sacrifice of Christ for us and sin against God Himself.[202]

So do we all clam up and say nothing of what we think for fear of offending God?

No. No one knows whom God will choose to inspire with words we all need to hear. And a priesthood doesn't serve its Lord by fearful silence or sullen inaction.

What we do is speak the truth—as we understand it—in love[203]—love for each other and love for God—if we are led to speak. And we speak our convictions in words and a spirit worthy

---

[199] Luke 24:15-16, 30-31.
[200] Romans 8:28.
[201] Matthew 19:26.
[202] Hebrews 10:26-29.
[203] Ephesians 4:15.

to be presented in God's presence, as sacred sacrifices offered to God, which they will be.[204] We listen with attention, patience, respect and love to all who choose to speak, as though it were God speaking through them, which may be exactly what is happening. And this is true whether we find the words, sentiments or reasoning to our liking or not.

We are all of us, together, God's church, God's people, God's possession, God's priesthood.

There is nothing like a church business meeting to cause God's people to forget who and what they are. Do not forget today. Remember who you are.

And because you are who you are, do as Peter says and *"put away all malice and all deceit and hypocrisy and envy and all slander"* and anything else that is not who and what God has called you and equipped you to be as the collective Body of Christ.

In short, do as Jesus commanded. When you come back into this room, *"love one another as [Jesus] has loved you."*[205]

That's about as practical as I can make it. Commence application immediately. Apply as often and as much as required.

☙•❧

---

[204] Psalm 19:14.
[205] John 15:12, RSV.

31.

Christ Suffered for Your Sins

1 Peter 3:18 NRSV

¹⁸ For Christ also suffered for sins once for all, the righteous for the unrighteous, in order to bring you to God. He was put to death in the flesh, but made alive in the spirit.

ॐ⋖

Christianity is the burr God has put under the world's saddle. Christianity is the sound of God's fingernails on the world's blackboard. God designed Christianity to rub the world the wrong way—wrong, from the world's perspective.

From God's perspective—and therefore, from the Christian's perspective—God (and we)—rub the world the "right" way. But either way, Christianity "rubs." It aggravates the world. And the world "rubs" back.

God is confronting—crowding—the world with the message of Christ *about* it, and the claims of Christ *upon* it. And the world is pushing back—pushing on the followers of Christ, since it can't actually "get at" Christ Himself (anymore).

Christians—when they are actually *being* Christians in the world—will suffer at the hands of the world—and by that, I mean the people who are *not*—and don't *want* to be—and don't even want *you* to be—Christians.

It's not that the world is so absolutely against good deeds, kindness or love. The world can tolerate a few good deeds, a little kindness, even what passes for love these days, assuming these things are kept within reason and motivated by nothing in particular.

But even good deeds can get you in trouble if you wrap them in the gospel or use them to demonstrate the difference between God and the world. Jesus was not crucified for being nice, but for being the One Who declared that the world wasn't.

Why is Christianity always at odds with the world? (And we should hope it always is.)

God wants it to be. God wants *us* to be. God wants to use us to be the salt and light that confront and challenge the moral indifference and spiritual complacency of the world.

But in the process, we suffer.

Now we're not talking about the normal, natural, everyday suffering that comes with drawing breath on this earth. We're not talking about the physical pain, mental anguish and practical setbacks every person experiences in life. We're talking about what you have to put up with because you are a Christian—what you could avoid if you were *not* a Christian.

That specifically "Christian suffering" is what Peter is talking about—talking a lot about. "Suffer if you have to," he says, "for being innocent, but not for being guilty of anything. And if you do suffer as a Christian—for *being* a Christian—for actively 'doing Christianity'—you're in very good company, because even though the world can't get to Jesus now, they did get to Him—big time!"

Do you suffer for Christ? Christ also suffered—for sin—for *your* sins—for *you*. Peter says (in the words of an early Christian hymn): *"Christ…suffered—for sins—once for all—the righteous for the unrighteous—in order to bring you to God."*

They packed a lot into one sentence, those early suffering Christians. Let's unpack it a little.

Christ suffered as a righteous man for the unrighteous—as an innocent man for the guilty.[206] His suffering, for us and for the world that caused it (and at the same time desperately needed it), was *vicarious* suffering.

Christ suffered for sins—to pay the fair penalty a just system requires if it is to remain just. His suffering atoned for—made up for—our sins and their sins—for all sins.

Christ suffered to bring you to God—a journey you *must* make but could not begin—let alone complete—on your own. His suffering was the bridge that spanned the gap between sinful humanity and its sinless God. Christ's suffering reconciled us to God.[207]

And this suffering—this vicarious, atoning, reconciling suffering of Jesus Christ—was done once for all. His suffering was sufficient—for all the world—for all time. He suffered for you and me and them.

And now, when—if—we suffer for Him, we suffer like Him.[208] Our suffering becomes vicarious, not because we are sinless like Jesus, but because we suffer for others, so that they may see Christ in our suffering.[209]

We suffer, not to atone, but so that by suffering like Him, we may point the unbelieving world to the One Who *has* atoned. We point, in our suffering, to the One Who, when lifted up on a Cross, draws all men to Himself.[210]

And so when we suffer for Christ, and with Christ, we may and should experience our suffering in humility, hope and joy[211] (as odd as that sounds to the world), because we know what God is doing

---

[206] Romans 5:6-8.
[207] 2 Corinthians 5:16-21.
[208] Philippians 3:8-10.
[209] Ephesians 3:13; Colossians 1:24-28.
[210] John 12:32.
[211] James 1:2-4.

with our suffering as Christians to reach all the other people who make up, with us, this broken, sinful world.

He suffered—once for all—the Sinless One for a world of lost sinners—for you and me and them—to bring us all to God. We know that He has accomplished, in His suffering, all that God requires for His suffering to be sufficient for them, too.

❧

Indices

Sermon Titles in Alphabetical Order

Sermon Titles in Alphabetical Order

Sermon Texts in Biblical Order

Related Sermons in Other Volumes

Additional Scriptures Referenced

Additional Scriptures Referenced

Additional Scriptures Referenced

Text	Title	Page

Additional Scriptures Referenced

Additional Scriptures Referenced

www.ingramcontent.com/pod-product-compliance
Lightning Source LLC
Chambersburg PA
CBHW020850090426
42736CB00008B/310